# HANDLING SERPENTS

# Handling
# SERPENTS

*Pastor Jimmy Morrow's Narrative History*
*of His Appalachian Jesus' Name Tradition*

## JIMMY MORROW
*with*
## RALPH W. HOOD, JR.
*editor*

Mercer University Press | Macon, Georgia | 2005

ISBN 0-86554-848-X
MUP/P302

First Edition.

The paper used in this publication meets the minimum requirements
of American National Standard for Information Sciences—
Permanence of Paper for Printed Library Materials, ANSI
Z39.48-1992

*Library of Congress Cataloging-in-Publication Data*

Morrow, Jimmy
Handling serpents: Pastor Jimmy Morrow's history
of his Appalachian Jesus' Name tradition
Jimmy Morrow; edited by Ralph W. Hood, Jr.
1st Ed.

p. cm.

Includes index
ISBN 0-86554-848-X (pbk.: alk. paper)
1. Snake cults (Holiness churches)—History
2. Church of God with Signs Following—History
I. Hood, Ralph W.
II. Title
BX7990.H6M67 2005
289.9–dc22

2005002195

# Contents

*I would like to dedicate this book to the memory of all the brothers and sisters in the lord that were martyred for the gospel of our lord Jesus Christ. They choose to suffer or die rather than renounce or give up their faith in Jesus Christ.*

*Jimmy Morrow*


*For my father, Major Ralph W. Hood*
*Ralph W. Hood Jr.*

# Preface

"And they went forth and preached everywhere, the Lord working with them, and confirming the word with signs following" (Mark 16:20).

# How I Came to Believe in Serpent Handling

The reason I am writing this book is to tell the truth of the five signs of the Bible as in Mark 16. I was called by God to preach the gospel of Jesus Christ with the signs following.

About fifteen years ago, at the age of fifteen, on a Sunday morning (it was sunny and the sky was clear and blue), I went to the pasture and caught my horse. I was going to ride on the mountain. I rode down the Old 15th and up toward Rocky Top. When I reached the old Fish Place, I stopped to rest my horse. It took an hour and a half to reach that place. I had stopped at Tinman Ball's store for a candy bar and a canned drink. After I ate, I got on my horse and started toward Low Gap Road that goes toward Hall's Top. I reached the triple fork of the road—one road went to Hall's Top, one went to Old River Road and the other went to Uncle Hall's house about 5 miles down. I wanted to go to Hall's Top but it was getting late, so I took the road that went past Uncle Hall's place. I passed the Old Bear Branch about three miles down the road. Right around the bend in the road, as the road leveled out, lay a large, yellow timber back rattlesnake with its rattlers up in the air. I was a sinner at the time and one thing I did not believe in was snake handling. My people had told me to stay away from people that handle serpents. They told me lie after lie about the Church of God and the saints that take up serpents.

One aunt had told me that they go to church and turn off the lights and get serpents out and handle them in the dark. She said they had a weed they ate and put on their hands so the snakes would not bite. My kinfolks also told me that the church members pulled the serpents' fangs so they would not bite, and they also told me they would take needles and thread and sew the snakes' mouths closed. I was young and believed all the stories that were told me and I grew to hate all the signs-believing people.

I sat there, looking at the rattler, telling myself that if the old Holiness people could handle a rattler so could I. I reached out with my hand and touched the rattler. In a lightning movement the rattler bit me twice on the left hand. It happened so fast, it was done in seconds. There I was, thirty minutes from anyone's house. I suddenly heard a voice telling me, "This time I will overlook your ignorance."

I looked at my hand and I knew that everything my kinfolks had told me was untrue. The Lord closed the serpent's mouth and it did not bite me again. I was a sinner and God let me live. The Lord could have let the rattler bite me again and I could have died on the mountain. But even though I was bit I was not hurt.

I got on my horse and went home. That was the summer of 1970 and five years later the Lord gave me a vision of hell. Since I want to first tell you about is the story of the Jesus' name handlers, I will tell you about the vision of Hell in Chapter 16.

The five signs of Mark 16:18 came again to God's people as evidence and testimony which furnish proof of the mighty power of God. Nearly 2000 years ago Jesus Christ told his disciples, "Go ye into all the world and preach the gospel to every creature. He that believeth and is baptized shall be saved; but he that believeth not shall be damned; and these signs shall follow those that believe, they shall speak in new tongues, they shall take up serpents, and if they drink any deadly thing it shall not hurt them, they shall lay hands upon the sick and they shall recover" (Mark 16: 17–18). These signs were given to his followers to confirm and to strengthen their faith. They would preach the gospel of the Lord Jesus, Christ would confirm His word by the signs following believers. This is the history of believers baptized In Jesus' name. That is why among serpent handlers were are know as Jesus' name people.

# Editor's Introduction

There are several excellent books on the serpent handlers of Appalachia, but none like this one. Here is a narrative of the Jesus' Name handlers by an Appalachian minister who practices a faith that outsiders have long stereotyped as an interesting but unfortunate form of worship, appealing only believers whose collective deprivations have been diagnosed as educational, cultural, and financial and whose psychological health has been questioned by more than one authority. The experts have described, diagnosed, and offered solutions to a form of religious expression whose very legality has been successfully challenged in a region noted for its colorful patchwork of diverse Christian convictions. Those reading such scholarly experts are likely to anticipate the disappearance of a tradition in which serpents maim and deadly poisons kill those who identify themselves as sign following believers.

Reverend Jimmy Morrow is one of these believers. His family roots, and those of his wife Pamela, run far and deep throughout the Appalachian Mountains that they both love. His story is both a personal narrative, telling of his conversion to the serpent-handling tradition, and a collective narrative telling the history of those who handle serpents and baptize in Jesus' Name. As Jimmy notes, any prediction of the obituary of this tradition is more than premature, it is a failure to understanding how Jesus' Name believers understand the Word of God.

Experts have explained away rather than explained this tradition. Jimmy Morrow is another type of expert. His history explores, even in the face of tragedies and suffering, a vibrant faith that is far from simple or simple minded. It is a faith that expresses a form of life in which the Bible is one's only sure guide. How that Bible is read, how it is preached will become evident as the complex history of this tradition unfolds. It is not a historian's history. Yet Jimmy's narrative cannot be dismissed. He is his own self-taught expert. His is a lived-knowledge of Appalachian culture by one who continues to help sustain a unique religious tradition. In the jargon of the social scientists, Jimmy's work is more than adequate as a reflexive ethnography in which the ethnographer and his ethnography merge not as an ethereal mysticism but as flesh and blood and an honest struggle with God's word.

To the academician trained in proper techniques of citation Jimmy's narrative has obvious flaws in terms of the proper identification of sources. He summarizes newspaper articles that he has clipped and pasted in numerous three ring binders over a period of thirty years. Most of these articles are yellowed with age and few have been cut so as to preserve dates or even titles of the newspaper in which they occurred. Jimmy's only concern was to save "stories," often of events he participated in. In true Appalachian style these stories are woven together with other oral reports and Jimmy's own personal experience to form a narrative history of the Jesus' Name tradition. Rather than to suggest Jimmy is trying to "document" his tradition as a professional historian would, I have chosen to identify his unique use of newspaper clippings by prefacing Jimmy's use of articles with a phrase, such as "a paper reported." Jimmy's use of clippings is, especially evident in chapters 8–14. Most clippings are obviously from the local papers in the towns in which the events being described occurred. If Jimmy had the date and/or newspaper name it is noted, otherwise only a generic reference to the use of newspaper articles is noted. It is for historians to identify the precise newspapers and dates in what are likely to be additional scholarly studies of a tradition that continues to fascinate scholars in the social sciences and in Appalachian studies.

My task has been to not interfere with Jimmy's story. I have compiled and arranged materials from sheets and scraps Jimmy has written and from the newspaper accounts Jimmy has either collected or recalled. Jimmy's love for his tradition is evident in how he utilizes clippings in conjunction with his ability to talk to people whose stories experts usually obtain only from the outside, or from interviews often carefully crafted by Appalachians who protect as much as they reveal about their culture. Jimmy is an Appalachian handler whose style remains what is distinctive about a culture that even when it acknowledges various media such as newspaper and television, cares most about taking whatever stories are told and making them part of their own.

This is Jimmy's history. It is his story. It is not of all handlers, nor is it the only history to be told. Yet it remains an essential history, a piece of the quilt that must be included in any effort to understand religion in the Appalachian Mountains.

I would not have encouraged Jimmy to tell his story if I did not believe as he does. I more than respect his beliefs and the source from which they come. I believe that if there is a sense to religious freedom, it is nowhere better expressed than from those who, in a simply act of obedience, handle serpents. I have heard it said more than once in small churches throughout Appalachia what now must be said in print: "If you do not believe in serpent handling, pray for those who do." Editing this book is my prayer for Jimmy, Pam, and all those who handle serpents in Jesus' Name.

Frank Necessary (left) and Kennth Short baptizing a sister
in Big Stone Gap VA

Opal Corn Myers and her three children with Morgan Gap
Mission in background

Oll McMahan (left) and Riley Arwood at Lord's Supper and foot-washing service at Sand Hill Church of God in Jesus' Name

Albert Morrow (1923–1968), son of Thomas Morrow and
Althea Bertie Fish and father of Jimmy Morrow

William Marion Fish (left), Laura Avaline Griffith (center),
and Minnie Fish (right)

Lawson Edward (back center) and Lou Ellen Russell Fish
and their children Aldan (back left),
Ira Bassum (front left), Cassie, Robert Lee (front right),
and Fidella Clingman Fish (back far right)

Euel Jacky Blackburn and mother at old Jess Turner House

 Pamela Morrow handling in service at Del Rio TN

Old Sand Hill Church of God in Jesus' Name, Del-Rio TN

 Marvin Turner, Pastor Sand Hill Church of God
in Jesus' Name

Della Mae Turner and Granny Blackburn (right)

Posey Rufus and Eveline Ford, with grandchild
(two years old)

The Morgan Gap Mission built in 1885. Known as "The Christy" Mission from Catherine Marshall's book *Christy*

 Liston Pack, pastor of Holiness Church of God in Jesus'
Name at Carson Springs from 1969–1992

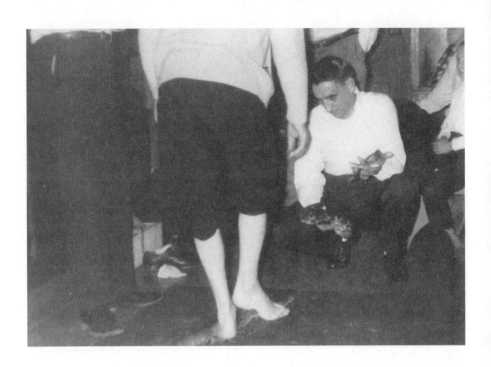

Lawrence Calloway walking on rattlesnake as James Brooks
handles, Big Stone Gap VA in 1940s

 Church service at Holiness Church of God in Jesus' Name,
Big Stone Gap VA in early 1940s

Jimmy and Pamela Ford at home in Del Rio in 1986

Rosco Mullins watching Earl Kilgore handle
at Big Stone Gap, VA in early 1940s

Wayne Coomer handling rattlesnake
at Big Stone Gap VA in 1940s

Jimmy Morrow's mother, Ruth Ellen Arrington,
holding her baby sister in 1939

Jimmy Morrow's grandparents, Tommy Morrow and Berdie
Fish Morrow, with children Walter (left), Zora (middle) with
Tom Green behind and Lawson (sitting on Berdie's lap)

Pamela Morrow's parents, John Ike and Bonnie Kate Pierce
Ford, with her sisters Imogene and Elizabeth (left)

Agnes Brooks and Rosco Mullins handling
in Big Stone Gap VA in 1940s

 Nancy Kleinieck handling serpents in arbor meeting.
Man with Bible is Jacky Blackburn. Photo from 1940

Jimmy Morrow in 1986 outside his home handling
copperhead

 Jimmy Morrow with serpent box and Ralph Hood outside
Jimmy's church in Del Rio TN (photo by Jeffrey Schifman)

Alfred Ball (left), Doyle Marsee, and Liston Pack (right)
handling in Carson Springs in 1969

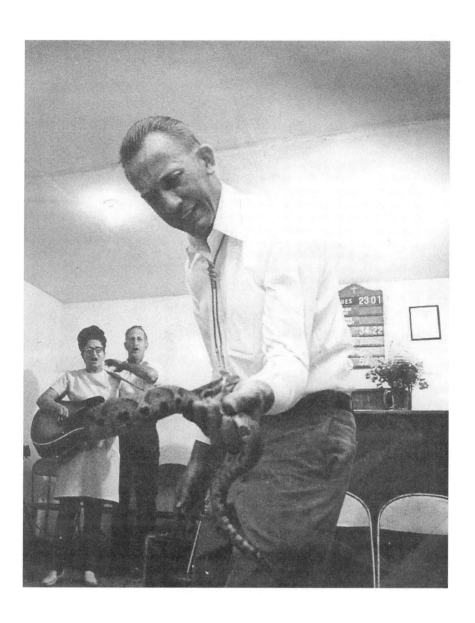

Jimmy Ray Williams handling serpent at Carson Springs
TN in 1969 while Beulah and Ed Arwood observe

Close-up of serpent

Jimmy Morrow handling at his church in Del Rio TN
(photo courtesy Jeffrey Schifman)

Nancy and William Leatherford,
grandparents of Jimmy Morrow

# Chapter 1

"My God, think thou upon Tobiah and Sanballat according to these their works, and on the prophetess Noadiah, and the rest of the prophets." (Nehemiah 6:14)

# The Doctrine of Jesus and the Prophetess Nancy Younger Kleinieck

Robert Fraley told me that his family was born in West Virginia. Lilburn Clark Fraley was born 1874 in Coal Wood. I heard them talk of outdoor meetings in Wise County, Virginia, during 1890–1900. There were many people at these meetings. The preachers had poles put into the ground and a plank nailed to the top of the pole to lay their Bibles on. They had boxes of serpents around homemade pulpits. All over the hills and in the valleys they preached. There would be hundreds of people at these open-air meetings. It was said that each preacher would be handling serpents and preaching to their congregation from sunup to sundown. The Farleys remember standing in the valley and looking around the hills while preachers would be handling deadly serpents. These were all Jesus' Name preachers. The rebirth of serpent handling was in Virginia and West Virginia.

During this time there was a family of Irish descendents. Their names were Emanuel and Susan Hensley and they had three children. They migrated into West Virginia. Susan Jane had another son that she named George Went Hensley. The Hensley family pulled up roots and migrated to Stone Creek, Virginia. This was in the 1890s.

During that time there the great coal-mine revivals were going on. Here is where George Hensley witnessed serpent handling almost twenty years before he was to pick up his first serpent at White Oak Mountain in Tennessee. The person he witnessed handling was the prophetess Nancy Kleinieck. She handled rattlesnakes and copperheads as she practiced the signs and preached the gospel of Mark 16. Hensley's witnessing the handling of serpents at Stone Creek never left his mind. Nineteen years later, when he handled his first serpent at White Oak Mountain, it was the memory Nancy Kleinieck that gave him the courage to obey Mark 16.

In 1860 Mrs. Younger had a daughter that she named Nancy. She lived in Stone Creek, Virginia, in a lovely settlement with its winding creek that was so blue it looked like the sky above had fallen and become liquid. The creek bottom was stone. It was this blue rock stone that gave the water its color.

During the Civil War, the Younger family had to try to get through the valley and mountains to find a way to earn a living. At that time there was slavery. The slave owners had the slaves work plantations around Charleston, Virginia, where they grew cotton and tobacco. All the hard work was done by African slaves who were bought and sold like some kind of animal or beast or horse.

Mountain folk say the way slavery got started was when a man who was too lazy to work saw ants captured and forced to work for other ants. If ants can do this, why not man? So the Negro was forced into slavery. As slaves came down Stone Creek Valley, they saw a big stone shaped like the face of a man. The white man said it is called "Nigger Rock." When the slaves passed the rock, they would bow their heads and weep. After the war "Nigger Rock" was changed to "Stone Face Rock."

When the war was over, the Younger family was trying to get back to normal. It was 1866 and squatters would settle on land without paper or title. They would settle on public land to acquire ownership under government sanction.

When coal was found in the hills of Virginia, people came from all over to work in the mines. Coal mining was becoming a big commercial enterprise and coal camps emerged all over the mountains. The miners lived in tents or huts and other shelters as the coal was taken from the earth.

It was in these coal camps that the families such as the Youngers, the Kleiniecks, the Smiths, the Grindstaffs, the Fraleys, the Wells, the Kilgores, the Spears, the Pelfreys, the Meyers, and the Misers worked and lived. The Youngers and the Klieniecks were the first to heed the call of God as Jesus' Name serpent handlers. Younger and Klienieck both handled serpents. The Youngers noticed a change that had come upon their daughter, Nancy. As a child she would go into the mountains and pray. The Youngers noticed that she was becoming a prophetess. She married Klienieck and it is as Nancy Younger Klienieck that she is known in the Jesus Only tradition as a prophetess of God.

Nancy Younger Klienieck was a young woman and a Jesus prophetess. She prophesized in the Jesus' Name doctrine and as it says in the Acts. She was a Jesus' Name serpent-handler. This was long before George Hensley handled serpents at White Oak Mountain. He was not the first to handle as many people have said. Prophetess Nancy believed in Ephesians 4:4–5: "There is one body, and one Spirit, even as ye are called in one hope of your calling. One Lord, one faith, one Baptism." This is the Jesus' Name doctrine that Nancy Younger preached.

Nancy often spoke from inspiration. She would utter things in prophecy. Scoffers would bring serpents by the boxful and she would handle them as the Lord moved upon her. She handled large serpents, many over 4 feet long and as big around as a man's arm. She did this during the coal-mine revivals started in the late 1890s and continued into the early 1900s. As the Lord Jesus moved upon her she would hold open-air meetings in the mountains of Tennessee, Kentucky, both Carolinias, and Virginia. As believers came out of Stone Creek, huge crowds would be formed. Some walked to the meeting site; some rode horses; some came on wagons pulled by terms of mules. As they gathered, the valley was filled with the saints of Jesus. After the death of the prophetess Nancy Klienieck, most of the outdoor meetings ended. Still serpents were handled and the gospel was preached in houses around and about.

During the same time, Oscar Hutton from St. Charles, Virginia, was also a Jesus' Name preacher. As a young man he was also handing serpents in 1890–1900 when Prophetess Nancy Younger Klienieck was handling. Later, in the great mine revival in the mountains of Virginia in the 1950s, before the death of Lee Valentine, Oscar held a meeting near the Tennessee, Virginia, and Kentucky state line. Oscar Hutton was an old man then. After the death of Lee Valentine, Oscar held a meeting as a memorial service for Lee that drew 250 serpent-handlers and 4000 onlookers. That service was one of the last great coal-mine revival meetings.

There was a traveling circus in the area. An elephant killed its trainer. The elephant was hung from a railroad underpass. People living then handed the story down mouth to mouth. They said you could see the elephant hanging from the railroad underpass. It was pulled up by a winch and hung with a steel cable.

When I was in Virginia I saw the large field where they use to have outdoor meetings and handle serpents. In the far background I saw a railroad underpass. Bob Fraley told to me that it was the same underpass that the elephant was hung on.

Vigal Q. Wax worked for *Life Magazine*. Dr. Axel Brett of the University of Tennessee was a psychologist. Wax wrote that this psychologist had said that snake handlers had a lot in common with people who do the jitterbug. He said accompanying the strange rites of the serpent handlers was the offbeat music of guitars playing old revival hymns and the tom-tom clapping of hands. There was also moaning and exhortations to "sweet Jesus," often accompanied by screaming in the unknown tongue. The psychologist claimed this was a frenetic gibberish to which the cultist resort when their religious fervor moves beyond intelligible speech. He called us glassy-eyed members of a religious cult. The people he was talking about were Jesus' Name people at Stone Creek. Vigal Wax and Dr. Axel Brett never said anything about who they where nor did they mention any of their names or even care who they were. For nearly sixty-two years nobody knew who the Jesus' Name people were in that *Life Magazine* article.

Twenty years ago Brad Richie sent me a 1940 copy of *Life Magazine* from Kentucky. Back in November of 2001, I was looking at it. There was a picture of an old woman handling a serpent, just a picture with no name. Over the years I have often wonder who she was and where she come from. Where did she live? I wonder if she was Jesus' Name or Trinitarian.

I know a Jesus' Name preacher nearly ninety years old. He was in poor health. His name was Robert Fraley and his son's name was Bob. Bob told him that a sister in the Lord left James Morrow a picture at his house. He called and asked if I wanted to go up with him to get the picture. I said yes. When we got there, Mrs. Fraley welcomed us in. She told us to have a seat and we did. She said she had a copy of the picture Louise Cress had given me. I opened the large envelope that she handed me and took out an 8"-by-10" photograph. As soon as I looked at it, I knew it was the old lady in the *Life Magazine*. It is the first pictures of a serpent handler. The photograph was nearly sixty-two years old. Mrs. Fraley called her mother, Mrs. Fig. She told me the history that was handed down mouth to mouth in her family. She told me how *Life Magazine* had said such hurtful things about the serpent handlers. After that Mrs. Fig was done talking; I handed the phone back to Mrs. Fraley. She then called Louise Cress. Louise said she would call back. I didn't think she was going to talk to me. However, in about five minutes the phone rang. Mrs. Fraley picked it up. It was Louise Cress. Mrs. Fraley handed me the phone. Louise asked who I was; I told her that I was James E. Morrow from Tennessee. I told her I was a Jesus' Name preacher and that I pastored the Edwina Church of God in Jesus Christ's name. I told her I was trying to gather all the history of Jesus' Name churches before it vanished off the earth. She told me that the old lady in the picture was her grandma and she told me she was a prophetess and that her name was Nancy Younger

Klienieck. She told me she was Jesus' Name and that she would hold outdoor meetings. She told me the history that I have written above.

She said that the picture that was given to her grandma Nancy Younger Klienieck. She in turn gave the picture to her daughter who was the mother of Louise Cress. She didn't know the young man that was also in the picture. I recognized him. I told her it was Euel Jacky Blackburn. He was a Jesus' Name preacher at the Sand Hill Church of God in Jesus' Name in Del Rio, Tennessee. I knew his face from other pictures that I had seen. A good sister in the Lord at the Sand Hill Church of God in Jesus' Name in Del Rio named Gladys showed me a picture of Euel holding rattlesnakes in both hands. She also showed me a picture of old Lester Raines. He was a Jesus' Name preacher and my half uncle. He preached at the church in Sand Hill. The picture showed him holding two copperheads, one in each hand. The picture was taken in Tennessee at what looked to be an outdoor service. This picture was later destroyed by a house fire. If still here, the picture would be over sixty years old. It is said that Blackburn's father and mother took him to the outdoor Jesus' Name meetings in Virginia as a boy.

There is no doubt in my mind that George Went Hensley was the first Trinitarian to take up serpents. There is also no doubt in my mind that as a boy George witnessed the handling of the serpent in the great coal mine revivals in West Virginia and Virginia. I believe that Jesus' Name people took up serpents before the Trinitarian's did. History shows that the Trinitarians left the Jesus' Name tradition. The apostles and prophets accepted the doctrine of Jesus Christ himself as their chief cornerstone.

Louise Cress told me she has never seen a copy of the *Life Magazine* with her grandma in it. I copied the pages off and sent them to her. That was all the history she knew. I asked her if she knew where Nancy was buried. She said she didn't really know. She said it could be in Pennington Gap or maybe in Stoney Creek.

We need to keep in mind that it was Jesus' Name people that preached being baptized in the name of Jesus. The Jesus' Name serpents handlers during the late 1800s and the early 1900s were in West Virginia and in Virginia.

The first time that I meet Ulysses Prince was in Virginia at an outdoor meeting. Ulysses Prince built three Jesus' Name churches. One was in Duck Town. Another one was in Copper Town or Turtle Town in Tennessee not far from Blue Ridge Mountains of Virginia. Handling serpents was done at these churches in the 1940s. As soon as the great coalmine outdoor revivals were over, people started to build churches. They built the churches so the law could not find them. The law could not hassle what it could not see. Persecution by the law was one of the reasons serpent handling went from outside meetings in fields and brush arbors to inside meeting in churches.

In his old days Ulysses Prince built a Jesus' Name church in Georgia. Serpents were not handled at this church. Prince had given up the practice in the early 1980s. It is interesting to know that all Jesus' Name churches were in West Virginia. The churches of the Lord Jesus, and at one time the biggest congregation of Jesus' Name people, was at a church in Lego West Virginia. At that time Ray Stewart had a congregation of 400 members. There was a church that was Jesus' Name in Scrabble Creek, West Virginia. Later Ed Turner pastored that church. It was closed down after his death. The flood of 2000 washed the building away.

Bishop Kelly Williams had a Jesus' Name church in Inmicco, West Virginia, and a Jesus' Name church in Columbus, Ohio. There was a Jesus' Name serpent-handling church in Alabama turn of the twentieth century. Nobody knows how it got started there.

All Jesus' Name churches that are in Tennessee and handle serpents came out Virginia. Today there is a Jesus' Name a church that still handles serpents is in West Virginia. There are no longer any Jesus' Name churches in Virginia that handle serpents. In the early 1900s, when the Big Stone Gap, Virginia, holiness church in Jesus' Name was organized, there were several churches associated with it. One was in Kingston, Tennessee, another in Morristown, Tennessee, and a third one in Del Rio, Tennessee.

After the death of Oscar Pelfrey the holiness Church of God in Jesus' Name at Sand Hill stopped the practice of the handle of the serpents in their services. They told the churches that were organized under them to also stop handling serpents. This caused some members to break off from the Sand Hill Church and to start new churches that still preached the signs and handled serpents. The Holiness Church of God in Jesus' Name was organized in Carson Springs. They handle serpents there with Jimmy Ray Williams as pastor.

Buford Pack married Kate Darneil; her father built a church in Marshall, North Carolina. It is called the House of Prayer in Jesus Christ's Name. The Holiness Church of God in Jesus' Name and the Marshall church work together.

Floyd McCall and Lester Ball pastored the Holiness Church of God in Jesus' Name at Greenville, South Carolina, where Floyd McCall pastored a Jesus' Name church. Lester Alfred Ball pastored a Jesus' Name serpent-handling church at Cosby, Tennessee; Carl Porter pastored the Holiness Church of God in Jesus' Name at Kingston, Georgia. He later renamed it the Church of the Lord Jesus Christ.

All the Jesus' Name churches in Kentucky were organized from Virginia. Tommy Coots went to the Old Bottom Church of God in Jesus' Name in Big Stone Gap, Virginia. He came back and built a church in Middlesboro, Kentucky, on land donated by Mrs. Turner. The name of the church is the Full Gospel Tabernacle in Jesus' Name.

Later Pete Rowe built a church in Baxter, Kentucky. He named it the Church of the Lord Jesus Christ. Pete Rowe told me that as a young boy his father, Pete Rowe, Sr., would box up serpents and go to outdoor meeting in Virginia to handle serpents. Pete Rowe and Jamie Coots were working together.

The Coots in Middlesboro changed their church name to the Church of the Lord Jesus Christ.

When Pete Rowe's sister got bit, he stopped the handle of the serpents in the church at Baxter, Kentucky. Jamie and Pete had a falling out over the handling of serpents. While John Brown, Jr. (Punkin), was still alive he persuaded Jamie Coots to change the church name at Middlesboro back to the Full Gospel Tabernacle in Jesus' Name.

All these churches got their teaching on Jesus' Name from the Big Stone Gap, Virginia, Holiness Church of God in Jesus' Name. The Big Stone Gap, Virginia, holiness churches got their Jesus' Name preaching during the great coal-mine revivals. Oscar Hutton from St. Charles, Virginia, was going to a Jesus' Name church in Durham, North Carolina, called Zion Tabernacle. The Jesus' Name people in Durham were violating city law by handling serpents. Colonel Hartman Bunn was the pastor of the church. Some of the Jesus' Name people were in jail with Colonel Bunn for handling serpents. At the Zion Tabernacle Church in 1948, a snake-handling convention drew Jesus' Name believers from Kentucky, West Virginia, Tennessee, and Virginia. There were over 1500 people at this service. *Life Magazine* sent a photographer to cover the convention. In the same year the Dolly Pond Church of God with Signs Following was handling serpents, a Trinitarian church was also violating the law by handling serpents in Tennessee. These two churches just a state apart, one a Trinitarian and one Jesus' Name, both handled serpents in violation of the law. While in jail in Newport, Tennessee, Euel Jacky Blackburn told the reporter that he was in *Life Magazine*. He also told the reporter that Emanuel Hensley and Susan Jane Hensley lived in West Virginia. He said their son George Went Hensley was born in West Virginia in the 1890s and that he might have first witnessed the handling of the serpents as a boy before their family moved to Tennessee.

There's no doubt in my mind that George Went Henley was the first Trinitarian to take up serpents. However, the rebirth of the Jesus' Name doctrine and the Jesus' Name snake handling came out of Virginia and West Virginia. The Lord called prophetess Nancy Younger to prophesize and to handle serpents in the name Jesus. I believe that the Jesus' Name doctrine holds the Truth and the Key to salvation. The Bible says, "Neither is there salvation in any other: for there is none other name (Jesus) under heaven given among men, whereby we must be saved" (Acts 4:12). The single name of Jesus is one and no more. The name of Jesus is joy in the souls that know him. Jesus is honey to the tongues of them that love his Name. The name of Jesus is sweet music to those that love to hear his name.

The Bible also says, "And I say unto thee, that thou art Peter, and upon this rock I will build my church; and the gates of hell shall not prevail against it. And I will give unto thee the keys of the kingdom of heaven: and whatsoever thou shalt bind on earth shall be bound in heaven: and whatsoever thou shalt loose on earth shall be loosed in heaven" (Matthew 16:18–19).

In Acts 2:38–39 the Bible says, "Then Peter said unto them, 'Repent and be baptized every one of you in the Name of Jesus Christ, for the remission of sins, and ye shall receive the gift of the Holy Ghost. For the promise is unto you, and to your children, and to all that are afar off, even as many as the Lord shall call.'" This is why James E. Morrow and other church members organized the Edwina Church of God in Jesus Christ's Name.

The headquarters at Big Stone Gap, Virginia, and my church are independent from one another now. They have their own congregation and I have mine. The Morristown House of Prayer in Jesus' Name and the Marshall Church in North Carolina called the House of Prayer in Jesus Christ's Name have changed the Jesus' Name doctrine. They preach that Christ is the Father's name. This has caused more a falling out among us. The Bible plainly states in 1 John 4:41, "And he said unto him we have found the messiah which is being interpreted, the Christ" (Christ means the anointed one). Jesus said in John 5:43, "I am come in my Father's name." In Matthew 1:21 it says, "And she shall bring forth a son, and thou shalt call his name JESUS." In

Matthew 1:25, the Bible says, "And he knew her not till she had
brought forth her firstborn son: and he called his name, Jesus."
Luke 2:21 reads, "his name was called JESUS, which was so
named of the angel before he was conceived in the womb."

During the 1940s, my grandpa and grandma worshipped with
the Trinitarians at the Codgill Chapel Memorial in the old 15th
in Del Rio, Tennessee. Lester Raines's family also belonged to
that church. One weekend he got up and preached the Jesus'
Name doctrine and the handling of serpents. They so opposed
the Jesus' Name doctrine they had a meeting the following
Wednesday at the church. The elders voted him out of the
church because he preached that "they shall take up serpents" as
it says in Mark 16:18 and that they must be baptized in the name
of Jesus as it says in Acts 2:38.

A Trinitarian church was going to donate their old pews to a
Jesus' Name church. However, when the Trinitarian church got
their new pews, a woman got up and refused to let them give the
old pews to our church because it was a Jesus' Name church. I was
told that some of the same people in the Trinitarian church said
that I put the snake on my mother. What actually happened is
that my mother accidentally stepped on a snake and got bit while
going to the creek. I actually was in Kentucky at the time. They
said I put the snake on my own mother because I was a Jesus'
Name preacher. A boy in a church, Bernie, told the church years
later that Lester Raines preached that if you do not believe Jesus'
Name you will go to hell. After that my grandpa Kelse told the
church that same day after Bernie left church he snagged a
rattlesnake with a fishhook. He pulled it up on a bank. He killed
it and said, "This is not how to handle a snake." I don't know if
he said that because Bernie said that Lester preached Jesus'
Name or hell. Sometimes it makes a person wonder if people are
following Jesus or man.

This is an interesting story about how Lizzie Taylor heard
her first Jesus' Name preaching. She is an elderly lady in her
eighties today. She goes to the Pineville Church of God in
Kentucky. It is the old Lee Valentine church on Right Fork

Road. It was the first serpent-handling church that George Went Hensley pastored. Saylor and Browing also preached there.

While people know about Right Fork, Left Fork has a little-known history. When you get to the big Y in the road and there is a church on the Right Fork Road that was built in the early 1900s. This is in Jenson, Kentucky, and today Homer Cox is the pastor. They still handle serpents at this church.

Over the years as time changed, a car lot was built in front of the church on Right Fork Road. It is built in front of the church. The church has a right of way, so the owner of the car lot has to leave the lot open all the time so people can go to the church. At a place called Thousand Sticks, Kentucky, there it is old plank church built out of yellow poplar. This church has been there as long as anyone can remember. Lizzie Taylor's mother went to this church as a young woman. The preacher was a young man from Virginia with the last name Hutton. It could have been Oscar Hutton as a young man.

He preached being baptized in Jesus' Name, the taking up of serpents, and about receiving the Holy Ghost. Lizzie Taylor did not have the Holy Ghost. She repented and was baptized in Jesus' Name. That same week she was doing her chores. While going after the cattle she prayed to Jesus and she got the Holy Ghost. She prayed about serpent handling. She saw a vision of the young Jesus' Name preacher. He was handling a big black rattlesnake. The rattlesnake's head turned into a baby's head and then back. Lizzie knew that by the power of the Holy Ghost serpents would be like a baby and would not hurt you. The following week, she went to church, but she doubted her interpretation of her vision. A young woman was handling a rattlesnake in the front of the church. It bit the woman. The woman had a baby. While the woman was recovering from the bite, Lizzie took care of the baby. A voice spoke to her and said, "Did the baby hurt you?"

Charlie Hall had a church in Hat Creek, Alabama. He was old at the time. As a young man he had been in the outdoor meetings in Virginia in the early 1900s. In the late 1980s, a huge canebrake rattlesnake killed him. He was preaching and went to the serpent

box. He reached in and got the canebrake out. It immediately bit
him and killed him. The canebrake was given to Billy
Summerford. It was so mean that nobody could handle it. Billy
named it "Satan." Gene Sherbert and Barry Crawford, a Jesus'
Name preacher, went to Billy's house to see it. Gene looked at it
in the locked serpent box. He asked Billy for the key to the lock.
Gene opened it, reached in, and pulled the big canebrake rattler
out. He handled it in the name of Jesus. Barry also handled it in
name of Jesus. It is the name of Jesus that the signs of the gospel
are done.

# Some Basic Facts About the History of Serpent Handling

Susan Jane Hensley and her husband Emanuel Hensley lived in West Virginia.

Their son George Went Hensley was born in West Virginia.

The Hensley's moved from West Virginia in the late 1800s.

During that time a great coalmine revival was going on in Virginia and West Virginia.

Jesus' Name preaching and Jesus' Name serpent handling were also going on during that time.

During that time Nancy Younger Klenieck was holding outdoor meetings as the Prophetess of the Lord Jesus.

*All* Jesus' Name Doctrine came out of West Virginia and Virginia.

The Hensley's lived in West Virginia. They left West Virginia for St. Charles, Virginia, in the late 1800s. This was where George Went Hensley may have first witnessed the handling of serpents as a boy in the period from 1890 to 1900.

Nancy Younger Kleinieck is in one of the oldest pictures of a serpent handler. (The picture in *Life Magazine* is over sixty years old)

The Hensley's moved from St. Charles, Virginia, and settled in Tennessee.

George Hensley had his wife, Amanda read Mark 16:17–18 to him. It is likely that he remembered witnessing serpent handling as a boy.

George Went Hensley went to White Oak Mountain in the early 1900s where God gave him the power of to handle a black rattlesnake for the first time.

George Went Hensley was the first Trinitarian to handle serpents.

Proof that George Went Hensley was a Trinitarian is that he was
given an Evangelist Certificate in the year 1919 from the
Church of God headquartered in Cleveland, Tennessee. It was
signed by the Overseer of the Church of God, A. J.
Tomlinson.

"Preach the word: be instant in season, out of season, reprove,
rebuke. Exhort with all longsuffering and doctrine." (2
Timothy 4:2)

# Chapter 2

"Preach the Word: be instant in season, out of season; reprove, rebuke. Exhort with all longsuffering and doctrine." (2 Timothy 4:20

# George Hensley and the Notoriety of Serpent Handling

We have already seen in the first chapter how the followers of Jesus again knew the evidence, which furnishes proof, with the prophetess Nancy Younger Klenieck. We noted how George Hensley witnessed handling as a young child. Thus, George was not the first person to handle serpents as many authorities claim. However, even though George Hensley was not the first person to handle serpents, he certainly was one of the most notorious and well-known of modern serpent handlers.

George Went Hensley was born in Tennessee in 1877. His religious background is unknown. In 1909, he was approximately thirty-two years old. On a hot, summer day in late June or early July, he was led by the spirit of God to the top of White Oak Mountain, about 30 miles from Chattanooga, Tennessee. Mark 16:18 had caused him much spiritual unrest—especially the part that said they shall take up serpents. Climbing up the mountain, many thoughts must have run through his mind. He knew that a bite from a rattler could kill him in minutes, but he also knew that God had commanded those who believe to take up serpents. Surely fear was in his mind as he reached the top of the mountain. His heart must have been pounding and sweat must have been pouring down his face. He likely was tired as he reached the top. When he got to the top his faith in Jesus Christ was stronger than all of his fears. It was stronger than even his fear of death.

There was no doubt in his mind that he could get bitten by a rattlesnake and die on top of White Oak Mountain where it might be days before anyone might find him. More important than this fear was George's desire for peace once and for all. George had never handled a serpent before, yet he believed if he was to receive spiritual rest after death, he must do so. The Bible told him so.

In the head of White Oak mountain is a huge rock. The rock is all different colors—red, blue, green, and pink. The early settlers gave it the name Rainbow rock. There is a huge gap in the side of the Rainbow rock. It was in that gap that George found what he had sought—a large, timberback rattlesnake. The reptile was coiled with its head back, ready to bite. Its rattle was rattling a blood-chilling warning, ready to kill with its deadly venom. George knelt on the ground a few feet from the rattlesnake, praying loudly to Jesus Christ. His face was upturned to the sky. He was asking Jesus to remove his fears and to anoint him with the Holy Spirit and his power. Suddenly, with a shout he leaped forward and grasped the serpent and held it in his trembling hands without getting bit.

The same day he carried the rattler in his hands for 10 miles, to the Church of God, in a small town in Tennessee called George Town, about 30 miles from Chattanooga in Grasshopper Valley.

The church was built in early 1908. Hensley was the pastor at the time he carried the rattler into the church. Hensley preached salvation through and by Jesus Christ. With the rattlesnake in his hand, he preached that signs would follow the believers. Members of the church got anointed to handle the serpent. Enoch Harden and Mark Bradden got anointed and handled the serpent and passed it among the rest of the people at the service. No one was bitten. After the service Hensley carried the rattler home. God's people had had victory over the serpent.

The five signs had again become known to Jesus Christ's followers in this small Church of God in Grasshopper Valley, Tennessee. Once again, as in the times of the Apostles, Jesus Christ would confirm the Word with signs following to his true believers.

George Hensley was a strict fundamentalist. He believed that the words of the Bible were inspired by God and should be believed and followed literally. The church members were forbidden things like drinking, smoking, immodest dress, and the cutting of women's hair as they still are today. We are God's people and, like holiness people, our lives reveal obedience to God in all things, including how we appear to others.

George Hensley held service in the Grasshopper Church of God for ten years. The church was growing rapidly because the signs were following the believers once again as they did in the days of the Apostles. Service after service, year after year, Jesus Christ would anoint the believers as they open the wooden boxes holding the rattlers and copperheads. The anointed would reach into the boxes and bring out the deadly serpents. They handled them, in the name of Jesus Christ. People would come from far and wide to the church in the valley to hear the gospel of Jesus Christ and to see the signs that would follow the believers.

During the services in the early 1900s, Hensley was having a service in the Grasshopper Church of God. After the service that night, Hensley started waking to his home. It took him an hour to walk to his house. It was a small roughly-built cabin. As he started to enter in the cabin, there were two men hiding inside the cabin. (I will identify them only by their initials, L. H. and S. H.). As Hensley went in the door. J. H and S. H. grasped him and held tight. One man was holding Hensley while the other man took a pocketknife and laid the opened blade to Hensley's ear. He slashed all the way down to the edge of Hensley's mouth. Blood was running down Hensley's face and pounding up off the floor. One man took another sweeping, slashing stroke, cutting Hensley stomach from side to side. Then the other man turned Hensley loose. Hensley fall to the floor in a pool of blood. As he lay there the two cutthroats took the knife once again and slashed clean across Hensley's back. Then J. H and S. H. left him for dead. The next morning some friends and relatives found Hensley, near dead, laying on his cabin floor. Blood was everywhere, but by the miracle of God, Hensley was still alive. They took him to one of their homes and washed the blood off of him. They doctored his wounds. Hensley recovered, but it took many months. It says in Romans12:19, "Dearly beloved, avenge not yourselves, but rather give place unto wrath; for it is written, 'Vengeance is mine; I will repay, saith the Lord.'" How true this is! J. H. died a sinner man. S. H. went crazy for what he had done to Hensley, a preacher of the gospel.

Mark Braddan was a great preacher of the gospel; his occupation was a blacksmith. Mark made tools and shoe horses for a living; his blacksmith shop and home was about a half a mile from the church. For ten years (from 1909–1919), Hensley held services at the church in Grasshopper Valley. Often the meeting was held outdoors. In the outdoors, services are called brush harbor meetings. At what turned out to be the last brush harbor meeting in Grasshopper Valley, there was large, black timberback rattlesnake. There also were several church members present. Garland Defriese opened the box, reached in, and picked up the serpent. As he was handling the serpent, the rattler fastened its fangs to Defriese's hand with a lightning movement. He fell to the ground at the feet of the other worshippers, with the fangs of the rattler still embedded in his hand. As he writhed in agony on the ground, the other believers began raising their voices in prayer toward heaven. They took him home where he recovered after a few weeks. However, the tragedy was such that they're no more meetings in Grasshopper Valley for twenty-three years.

People began to persecute Hensley and the members of the church in Grasshopper Valley. So most of the member said they did not want the signs of the gospel in their church anymore. They told Hensley and those who supported him to stay out of their services. They did not want Hensley as a pastor any longer. In Luke 21:12 the Bible say, "But before all these, they shall lay their hands on you, persecute you, delivering you up to the synagogues, and into prisons, being brought before king and rulers for my name's sake."

George Went Hensley left Tennessee that same year (1919) and started a new church in Pine Mountain, Kentucky, 17 miles south of Harlan, where he continued handling serpents. Even though there were no more serpents handling in Tennessee for many years they still preached that the signs would follow the believers. They knew that the Word is still the Word; that the Word of God cannot be changed.

The church that Hensley founded in Pine Mountain was also called the Church of God. He found another pastor for the church that he founded so he would be free to evangelize all over Kentucky. He preached in Harlan, Middlesboro, Louisville, Pineville, and Blackmont. Everywhere he preached, new churches were formed. There had different names such as the Pentecostal Church of God and the Pineville Church of God both in Pineville, Kentucky. The Pineville Church of God was founded in 1931. Two years later, Reverend Brown began handling serpents and the church has done so for fifty-two years, with the exception of six months back in late 1982 or early 1983. Reverend Brown and his wife were both in their eighties. They died of natural causes. Their son is now the preacher of that church. In fifty-two years of serpent handling, only one member has been bitten. That was in 1940. At that particular service, Reverend Brown requested that no serpents be brought to the service because there was confusion among the members in the church. A man defied Reverend Brown's request and brought a snake in anyway. He was bitten. Members took him home where he died a few years later. Anytime there is confusion in a church or among its members, it is best if there are no serpents brought to the church for handling.

## Chapter 3

"And there were many lights in the upper chamber, where they were gathered together" (Acts 20:9).

# The Jesus' Name Churches Organize and Grow

In the 1920s, Hensley traveled through Virginia as an evangelist, preaching the true gospel of Jesus Christ with the signs following the believers there. At that time the best-known, serpent-handling church in the state of Virginia was the Holiness Church of God in Jesus' Name. It was well organized and the headquarters of all the rest of the churches in Virginia. During the 1920s, the pastor was Earl Smith of Appalachia, Virginia. The assistant pastor was Cecil Grindstaff of Roda, Virginia. The deacons were Robert Fraley, Ivory Wells, Earl Kilgore, and Chester Spears, all of Big Stone Gap, Virginia.

The Holiness Church of God in Jesus' Name was the name of the association of churches with preachers working together for the publishing of newsletters and teaching the true gospel. The chairman of the board was Reverend Sam Clifton of Inboden, Virginia. Other officers included Myrel Sturgill, treasurer and Robert Fraley who was secretary and head of Enrollment for Membership of Pastors. Reverend Clifton was presiding bishop. The preachers were Reverend Sam Clifton, Reverend Earl Smith, Reverend Cecil Grindstaff. Most of the preachers came from cities in Virginia like Reverend Frank Necessary from Roda and Reverend Oscar Pelfery from Big Stone Gap. However, some came from Tennessee such as

Reverend Bill Myers of Kingsport and Reverend Myrel Miser of Morristown. There were several churches in other states that were associated with this headquarter church in Big Stone Gap.

In 1947, several states began to make laws against serpent handling. Six members of the Church of God in Jonesboro, Virginia, were jailed for the handling of serpents in violation of the new state law against serpent handling. In 1979, there was still a serpent-handling church in Rose Hill, Virginia, despite laws against the handling of serpents. As far as is known, no one has been bitten at that church until Dwayne Long received a fatal bite on Easter Sunday 2004.

In 1918 in Big Gap, Virginia, a church was built in the bottomland. It was named the Holiness Church of God in Jesus' Name. The church was built out of yellow poplar. Often many people attended this church. At one church service there were hundreds of people. There were people in from several states. Boxes of serpents were stacked seven high, all around the front of the church and about the pulpit. Each box had three to four rattlesnkaes in it. The Fraleys, Grindstaffs, Smiths, Spearss, Kilgores, Sturgils, Cliftons, Necessarys, Misers, and Ivory Wells were all in attendance. Oscar Pelfrey and his family were also there. The services got started with singing and shouting and dancing in the power of the Lord. Ivory Well got down the serpent boxes one at a time. He took out the serpents one by one and laid them on the floor in front of the pulpit. When Wells got all the serpents out there were hundreds of rattlesnakes just laying there all over the floor. They just laid there and did not move. Wells handle every one of then before he put them back in the boxes. It was a service to remember! All the serpents were handled with victory. Nobody was bitten. However, at the afternoon service a redheaded man named Johnson went to snake box and got a big black rattler out. It immediately bit him. He passed out and had to be carried out of the church. A sister spoke and said, "It might be your time," but the Lord said it was not his time. Johnson come back for the evening service and every serpent that was at the church meeting was handle. Nobody was bit. Johnson was taken home. His hand and arm were swollen down in to his chest. He was black and blue. He recovered in a few weeks. This was in the early 1920s.

In August of 1968 in Harlan, Kentucky, the Short family was attending the Holiness Church of God in Jesus' Name at Big Stone Gap, Virginia. Kennth Short and his wife Bobby and his son Cameron. Kennth had a big black rattlesnake that he had caught a week before. He kept it along with other rattlesnakes in a den box in a shed in the back of his house. Before the church service he went out and got the rattlesnakes out and put them into a carry box. The big rattler was 4 feet long and as big around as a man's arm. They loaded up their old 1955 Ford and headed into Virginia.

That evening before the church service things were just not right. It was August 4, 1968. Kennth parked his car under an oak tree for its shade. He did not want the heat from the hot August sun to be directly on his serpents. He placed the serpent box on the back seat of his car and started toward the church. Once inside the church Kennth noticed that there was no serpents anywhere. Oscar Pelfery asked Kennth Short if he brought any serpents. Kennth said that he had two serpents in the back seat of his car. Oscar and Kennth went out of the church to Kennth's car and so that Oscar could look at the rattlesnakes. Oscar said he would like to take the serpents into the church. Kenneth told Oscar that something was just not right. About that time Mullins pulled his car up and parked it behind Kennth's car. Mullins got out and shook the hands of both Oscar and Kennth. Oscar got the serpent box from Kennth's car and all three walked into the church. Oscar took the serpents and set them down in front of the church. The church was full of people.

Monnie was among the people at church that day. She told what happened. Church started with prayer and singing. Then Oscar Pelfery got to preaching. He told the church to bring the sick and the lame and the blind to next week's service. It was going to be a healing service where everyone would be healed. Monnie said that Mullins was up front and was using his foot to push the serpent box toward Oscar. Mullins just keep doing it and finally Oscar opened the box and got one of the rattlers out. He began handling it. The serpent was crawling like it was trying to get out of his hand and crawled into the air. The serpent became real stiff and then all of a sudden it fell limp with its mouth wide open. It then suddenly leaped up and struck Oscar in the side of his head. It hung on his temple. The serpent was drooping from his face while the other part of the serpent was still in Oscar's hand. He pulled on the serpent, yanking the fangs out of his flesh. Monnie said you could see the fangs come out while the blood ran down Oscar's face. Oscar just stood and looked at the serpent. In a few minutes he let go of the serpent and it dropped to the floor. Mullins reached and got the serpent and put it back in the box. Oscar set down on a bench. He was taken home where he died eight hours later. The next day the news got to the Del Rio Church of God in Jesus' Name that Oscar had been bitten and was dead. T. D. Ball came to Ed Ball, me, and to my uncle while we were hanging tobacco in a barn in the hollow an told us that Oscar was dead. This was in August 1968.

At one evening service, the pastor, Reverend Austin Long, let one of the members, Brother Gary, deliver the sermon. One man sat at the front of the church with his feet propped upon a glass-top box, which contained a large, yellow rattlesnake. After the sermon, Reverend Long asked the congregation to lay hands and pray over a woman who had cancer. When that was done, the man that had his feet on the snake box got anointed and handled the snake. Two or three other members handled the snake, too.

Hensley had preached in the state of Georgia. At that time the best known serpent-handling church in Georgia was the Wade Chapel Church in Cartersville. While Luther Wade, the founder of the Wade Chapel Church, had heard Hensley evangelizing, and became convinced of the necessity of God's people to take up serpents. The church is still standing today and they still handle serpents in their services.

In August 1984, the pastor of the church was Richard Barrett. He was handling a serpent during a service and was

bitten. He was taken to a member's home. Sheriff Don Thurman
had been called and asked Reverend Barrett if he wanted the
ambulance. He said, "I put myself in the hands of the Lord. If it
is His will that I die, then so be it." He died nine that evening.
Sheriff Thurman's comment at that time was "What can you do
when a man gets bit by a rattlesnake and refuses treatment? It's
his right—it's his freedom of religion."

Somewhere in Kentucky, in 1935, Oscar Hutton was reading
the Bible in his home. He was reading Mark 16:18—in particular
he thought about "they shall take up serpents." "That does not
mean just any snake, he told his wife, that means poisonous
snakes." The following weekend, at the church where he was
pastor, he told the members (after preaching the signs of the
gospel) of the church that he wanted someone to bring him a
snake the following night. Oscar had never handled a serpent
before. Someone caught a large rattler and brought it to church
the following night. At the service, Oscar opened the box and got
the rattlesnake out. Almost immediately it bit him on the right
hand. After the service, Oscar's arm was badly swollen and turned
blue. A few days later, as Oscar was recovering at his house, a
doctor from the hills who had heard that Oscar had gotten bitten
came to the house and asked to see Oscar. He asked Oscar if he
wanted treatment and Oscar refused. The doctor then asked Oscar
what he would do if someone brought him another snake. He told
the doctor that he would handle it with his good hand. Shaking his
head in amazement, the doctor left.

During the late 1930s, in Hazard, Kentucky, George Hensley
and a man named Marsee went to a church where the pastor had
gotten bit by a rattlesnake and was sick. The first night at the
church there were only nine members left. During the following
week of services held by Hensley and Marsee, the church was
built back up to seventy-nine members. On the last night of
services, after Hensley had delivered his sermon, he went to the
serpent box. When the anointing moved upon him, he reached
into the box and pulled out a copperhead, which he handled in
the name of Jesus Christ. Marsee then took the snake from

Hensley. While Marseee was handling the serpent it bit him on the palm of the hand, but he felt no harm.

Years ago, in the1940s, Oscar Pelfrey was going from his home in Virginia to a church in Kentucky for a service. He had a rattler in his car that he had handled for about a year. He came to a wooded area and decided to let the snake loose. He took the snake box out of the car, walked over to a bank, and set the snake free. He turned and headed back toward the car. When he reached the car, he turned around and found that the snake had followed him back to the car. He picked up the rattler and put it back in the box and continued his journey. When he arrived for the service in Kentucky, a woman handled the snake. It bit her but did not harm her.

On November 20, 1985, in a Wednesday night service somewhere near Blackmont, Kentucky, Mark Daniel asked one of the members to bring up a serpent box. He opened the box and handled the snake. He called for a second box and repeated his actions. He asked for a third serpent box (It contained a rattlesnake that one of the women had handled earlier.), opened it, and was handling the snake when it bit him on the hand. He sat down and died a few minutes later. He was buried somewhere in Kentucky.

The first time I was in Georgia was on Saturday, May 29, 1982, at the Church of the Lord Jesus Christ in Kingston. It was a homecoming. I went with Brother Punkin Brown. We got there about four in the afternoon. We got a room at a hotel and left for church about six that evening. We got there about half past six. The service started at seven. Brother Gene Sherbert was the pastor at the time. He gave us a nice welcome and told us to obey the Lord. That night the church was full of people from five states—West Virginia, Virginia, North Carolina, Tennessee, and Georgia. There were also three reporters from New York—the service went worldwide. The service started with singing. After that, Brother Charles Prince read Job 26 and then got anointed to handle two large rattlesnakes. The anointing of Jesus Christ

moved on me to handle serpents and then the anointing moved
on everyone to take up the serpents.

There was a large rattlesnake lying on the pulpit when
Ulysses Gordon Prince reached out and laid his hand on the
pulpit. As he was praying the serpent started to crawl up his arm,
around his neck and down the other arm. The serpent stopped on
his hand and rested there for ten minutes. Then Brother Prince
got the serpent and laid it back on the pulpit.

Brother John Brown, Sr., preached that night. About ten
o'clock, Rayford Dunn went to the serpent boxes—he got two
large rattlers, three small rattlers, and two copperheads and a
cottonmouth. The Lord told him to put all the serpents into one
box. He put the two large rattlers into one box and started to put
the rest in another box but the cottonmouth moved like
lightning and bit him on the little finger. He seemed to be doing
fine as the service came to an end that night. We stopped for
something to eat before going back to the hotel. When we got to
our rooms, five or six brothers came to Rayford's room to pray for
him. He was doing fine until about six-thirty Sunday morning
when the snake venom was shooting pain all through his body.

We started to go home, but Rayford wanted to go to the
homecoming at the church. He was so weak when we got to the
church that we had to carry him in. There were a lot of members
already at the church, so Gene started the service. John, Gene,
and I prayed for Dunn—the pain would come and go. About
eleven-thirty victory came—Jesus Christ healed Rayford Dunn of
the serpent venom. Gene got a serpent out of the box and was
handling it, the anointing moved on me and Rayford to handle
the serpents. Rayford was shouting and praising the Lord for
healing his body. He did most of the preaching that day. Ulysses
Gordon Prince preached the closing message at the homecoming.
He preached out of the tenth chapter of St. John. Afterwards, we
had dinner and then about three in the morning went back to
Tennessee.

The second time I was in Georgia was May 28 and 29, 1983.
Brother John Brown went down on a Wednesday to start a revival

that would run five nights. My wife Pam and I did not leave for Georgia until Saturday. We first went to Whitepine, Tennessee, to Brother John Fish's house. We then drove to Georgia with him. We left his house about one in the afternoon. It took about three hours to get to Georgia. We got rooms and rested awhile before church that night. We got to the Church of the Lord Jesus Christ early—no one was there when we arrived. We got out of the car and sat down on some wooden seats that were outside. John Fish and I were talking and a few minutes later Carl, Jr., and John Porter drove up. John got out of the car and came over and started talking. Carl, Jr., drove away. Around 6:30 the brothers and sisters started arriving for the service. At that time there was no pastor for the church and Brother Carl Porter, Jr., was the general overseer of the church. There were people from five states there. The service started at seven that evening. Brother Brown started the service. The singers started to sing. Brother Charles Prince got anointed to handle the serpents. He got rattlers out of the box and the spirit of the Lord moved on Rayford Dunn to take up the serpents. Almost every brother was handling the serpents. Jesus Christ anointed me to walk on the serpents. There were about eight big copperheads laying on the pulpit. I got them and took off my shoes and laid them on the floor and walked on them. At that time John Fish took up a large rattler. That was the first time Jesus Christ let me walk on the serpents. A copperhead bit Brother Rayford Dunn, but Christ gave him victory over the serpent bite. He did not get sick or swollen. Brother Ralph Vauylm preached that night. The service ended at two in the morning. It had lasted for seven hours.

The next day services started at eleven in the morning. Brothers Perry Bettis and Glen Dukes (from Tennessee) were there. Brother Perry preached some and all of the brothers testified for the Lord. Jesus Christ gave victory over the serpents and Brother Brown preached from Ezekiel 34. Afterwards we had dinner and went back home to Tennessee.

Georgia had many serpent-handling churches. In 1984–1985 two homecomings were held at the Holiness Church of God in

Jesus' Name in Cader Cheek, Georgia, where Gene Shurbert was the pastor. There were also homecomings at House of Prayer in Jesus' Name in Rome, Georgia, where U. G. Prince was the overseer and Wade Chapel in Cartersville, Georgia, where James Wade was the pastor. Back in the thirties the founder of the Wade Chapel Church, Luther Wade, would place rattlesnakes in one big pile, take off his shoes, roll up his pants legs to his knees, and walk on them in the name of the Lord. Sometimes the serpents would bite him, but he would feel no harm.

In 1946, in Calhoun, Georgia, Gordon Miller handled two giant rattlesnakes without getting bit. However, through the 1940s several handlers died from serpent bites. The Jesus' Name people still believe in the signs in Mark 16 even now in 2003. In the 1947, when the first man-made law was passed against serpent handling, Oscar Hutton held a service at the Kentucky and Virginia line. There were 250 serpent handlers and 4000 people at that service. Jesus Christ gave victory over all the serpents. No one was bit. Oscar Hutton said there were at least 1000 serpent handlers in Harlan County alone at that time.

## Chapter 4

"But he giveth more grace. Wherefore he saith, 'God resisteth the proud, but giveth grace unto the humble.'" (James 4:6)

# Serpent Handling Comes to Grasshopper Valley

In the late spring of 1943, a serpent-handling preacher from Kentucky by the name of Raymond Hays came to Grasshopper Valley, Tennessee, to hold services. He brought a boxful of rattlesnakes and copperheads. Hays preached to the people, warning that unless they repented and believed in Jesus Christ and returned to the faith, they could not inherit eternal life. Hays got anointed to handle the serpents, opened the box and brought out two rattlesnakes and a handful of copperheads. The backsliding brethren repented their sins and stood up shouting. One by one, they took the serpents from Preacher Hays as the anointing moved on them. Young men and women who had heard their elders talk of having handled serpents were handling snakes themselves for the first time.

In Hensley's services, back in the early 1900s, sinners went down to the hand-hewn altars and received the Holy Ghost. They arose and took the serpents from repented fathers and mothers. Sometimes children handled in the early days. They were seldom bit, and even those bit were seldom hurt. No child has ever died from a serpent bite at one of our services. Today we no longer allow children to handle due to pressure from man-made laws.

Raymond Hays said these signs shall follow them who believe in the name of Jesus Christ. With the rebirth of serpent handling in Grasshopper Valley in the 1940s, they built a church which was named the Dolly Pond Church of God with the signs following. It was located along a dusty road where some of the brethren lived. It was their monument to renewed hope and a pledge to Jesus Christ to never weaken again. Their pastor, Tom Harden, got the calling in 1938 at the age of twenty-nine. He had never handled serpents until Hays's service in 1943 and he has been handling snakes ever since. He held services in Dolly Pond ever Saturday and Sunday night. When the denominational Church of God and the Church of God of Prophecy discontinued handling serpents, the Dolly Pond Church was torn down and a new non-handling church built. Some call us "renegade Churches of God," but we still follow the Word. It is the big denominational churches that have strayed from the truth. Down the road a piece from the old Dolly Pond Church is a small church where true believers still handle.

In the old Dolly Pond Church unbelievers from nearby communities challenged the members of Harden's church to see if Jesus Christ would anoint them and give them power over fire and serpents. During one such service a Baptist minister lit a blowtorch and told Harden to try it. Harden grinned broadly as the blue flame was spewing from the torch. One member, an eighty-year-old woman walked slowly to the Baptist minister, took the torch as the anointing moved her, and held her hand in the roaring flame. Without a word, she handed the torch back to the minister, who turned off the torch and quickly left.

Another time an unbeliever decided to make fun of the Word of God. He believed that the serpents the church handled were either defanged or milked of their venom. His chance came one day when he and a friend captured a live, 11-pound timberback rattlesnake in the mountains. That same night (Saturday), he put the rattler in a 5-gallon milk can and took it to the service at the old Dolly Pond Church. During the service that night as Tom Harden was preaching the gospel of Jesus Christ, the anointing moved on him to take that large rattler out of the milk can. He reached in the can and handled the serpent in the name of Jesus Christ. The anointing moved on more members and they, too, handled that huge snake. The unbeliever, a twenty-year-old man from the valley named Cecil Denkins, confessed that he believed that the members would either refuse to handle the snake or at least one of them would die from its bite. A few weeks later Cecil joined the church, got the Holy Ghost and with it the power to handle serpents himself.

Most church services start by the members greeting each other—sisters give sisters the holy kiss and brothers give brothers the holy kiss, then brothers greet sisters (and vice versa) by name and a handshake. After the greetings, the guitar and tambourine players start the service with singing. During the singing members will come up for prayer, for the anointing to move on them to heal the body. When the members feel the anointing move on them to handle the serpents, they do so. After this, the pastor gives the altar call. If any come up for prayer, they have prayer and the service is ended. In Revelation 14:13 it says, "And I heard a voice from heaven saying unto me, 'Write: Blessed are the dead which die in the Lord from henceforth.' 'Yeah, ' saith the Spirit, 'that they may rest from their labours; and their works do follow them.'" In Psalms 116:15 it says, "Precious in the sight of the Lord is the death of His saints." And in Matthew 16:24–25 the Bible says, "Then said Jesus unto His disciples, 'If any man will come after me, let him deny himself, and take up his cross, and follow me. For whosoever will save his life will lose it: and whosoever will lose his life for my sake shall find it.'"

The first member of the Dolly Pond Church that died for the gospel was Lewis F. Ford. In 1945, a few months before his death in September, he repented of his sins. He was the son of Walter Ford, a deacon of the church. He was appointed official reader for the pastor. Jesus Christ had given Lewis victory over the serpents many times. It was through Lewis Ford that the gospel of Jesus Christ with the signs following the believers reached the people living in Chattanooga during the summer of

1945. Ford was employed as a truck driver at a plant a few miles east of Grasshopper Valley. During work he would preach to the other employees about salvation through Jesus Christ and the signs following, about believers taking up serpents. His fellow workers were amazed and told their friends who passed the word on to a newspaper in Chattanooga. A reporter and photographer were sent to check on the unbelievable story and found that it was true. Pictures and official reports were sent over Associated Press, which reached nearly every American outpost in the Pacific, Europe, and Africa. A photograph of Ford handling a deadly rattlesnake was carried in a Chattanooga paper and Ford found that wherever he went he was singled out by others as a true believer in Jesus Christ.

Ford and some members were having a brush harbor meeting at Daisy, Tennessee. Ford was preaching the gospel of Jesus Christ with the signs following the believers. Several members were anointed to handle five or six large rattlers. Ford was handling a huge timber rattler when it bit Ford on his hand, the fangs deep in his flesh. His faith in Jesus Christ was strong, so Ford did not cry out nor did he release his hold on the snake but continued as if nothing unusual happened. But several members at the service had seen Ford calmly force the rattler's fangs from his hand and had seen the blood begin to ooze from two tiny holes. Minutes later, Ford began to stagger about on the platform as the rattler's venom began to take hold. He fell to the floor and the members, realizing that Ford was in danger, began to pray. Ford knew that his time had come. In 2 Timothy 4:6–8 the Bible says, "For I am now ready to be offered, and the time of my departure is at hand. I have fought a good fight, I have finished my course, and I have kept the faith: Henceforth there is laid up for me a crown of righteousness, which the Lord, the righteous judge, shall give me at that day: and not to me only, but unto all them also that love His appearing." Ford was carried to the home of an aunt by the members, who prayed around him on the cot which they had placed him. Ford died just seventy minutes later.

The report of Ford's death was carried the following day in the Chattanooga papers. An estimated 2000 people attended the funeral. Ford was well liked wherever he went. Two days after his death, they had his funeral at the old Dolly Pond Church of God. People came from Kentucky and Virginia. Raymond Hays conducted the service. At the service he handled six large rattlers in the name of Jesus Christ. After the service they buried Ford on the hillside near the church.

The Bible says in John 11:25, "Jesus said unto her, 'I am the resurrection, and the life: he that believeth in me, though he were dead, yet shall he live.'" The Bible also says in 1 Thessalonians 4:16, "For the Lord Himself shall descend from heaven with a shout, with the voice of the archangel, and with the trump of God: and the dead in Christ shall rise first." Ford died for the gospel of Jesus Christ and he had hope of resurrection at the second coming of Jesus Christ. In 1945, Ford reached more people with the gospel of Jesus Christ than most preachers would have done in fifty years. Ford was a great man of God.

Once George Hensley and Tom Harden took a rattlesnake inside the city limits of Chattanooga for a service. A man asked them to come to his house and have services. Hensley was preaching the gospel of Jesus Christ with the signs following the believers. A large crowd was at the service. Hensley got anointed to handle the serpents and he reached in the box and got the serpent out and handled it in the name of Jesus Christ. Tom got anointed to handle the serpent, also. Police arrived on the scene and arrested Hensley and Harden for preaching the gospel and handling the serpents. The police then shot the rattler.

Hensley was the most notorious person to handle serpents and many people think he was the first to handle. We have seen how this is not true in chapter 1. Yet in 1909 when God revealed the true gospel with the signs following to George, he went on to be the most notorious handler. Newspapers reported on his activities as he traveled across the Appalachians and the Southeastern states. Thirty-five years later he was on trial for the gospel. The Bible says in Mark 13:9, "But take heed to yourselves: for they shall deliver you up to councils, and in the synagogues ye shall be beaten: and ye shall be brought before rulers and kings for my sake, for a testimony against them." At the time of Hensley's and Harden's arrest, there was no law against serpent handling—this was in 1945.

In jail, they prayed and sang during the night. The Bible says in Matthew 5:10–12, "Blessed are they which are persecuted for righteousness' sake for theirs is the kingdom of heaven. Rejoice and be exceedingly glad for great is your reward in heaven, for so persecuted they the prophets which were before you." The following morning at the trial, presided over by Judge Martin A. Fleming, relatives and friends of Tom and George and members from the church were there. Hensley and Harden were fined $50 each for handling serpents and preaching the gospel. Money was hard to get in those days—they preferred to go to the workhouse where, at a dollar a day, they could pay the fines in two months. After several days of hard labor as members of a road gang, Hensley, at the age of sixty-eight, began to weaken under the hot sun. Hearing of his condition, friends of the elderly Hensley got an attorney and appealed the case. The appeal was heard before Judge Frank Darwin who dismissed the charges.

In the year 1946, another death for the gospel of Jesus Christ with the signs following occurred. Clint Jackson, at a service near Daisy, Tennessee, took up a large rattlesnake. It struck him on the hand. He died forty-five minutes later. The Bible says in Hebrews 9:27, "And as it is appointed unto men once to die, but after this the judgment." It also says in Ecclesiastes 3:2, "A time to be born, and a time to die, a time to plant, and a time to pluck up that which is planted." Members have to testify and to die in the signs. If they never handle a serpent, they still have to die some kind of death.

The report of Jackson's death during a religious service spread far and wide and so the state of Tennessee passed a law against serpent handling. It was directed against the Church of God and its practice of serpent handling. On February 4, 1947, a bill was introduced in the Senate and the House simultaneously by Willard Hagan and Representative I. D. Beasley calling for the passage of the following: "That it be unlawful for any person or persons to display, exhibit, handle or use any poisonous or dangerous snake or reptile in such a manner as to endanger the life or health of any person." Sponsors of the bill asked that the penalties for violation be a fine of $50 to $150 or a jail sentence of six months or both. On February 28, 1947, the bill to ban serpent handling, having already received Senate approval, passed in the House by a vote of 75-0. Governor Jimmy McCord signed the bill and now serpent-handling churches was now against the law. The news soon got to Grasshopper Valley. Members were saddened by the law and gathered at the home of their pastor. Preacher Harden asked the oldest member of the church, Mark Bardam (who was in his eighties) what he thought of this new law. Bardam answered in a feeble but determined voice that there is only one lawgiver and that is Jesus Christ. Then he read from Mark 16 and the members began shouting and speaking in tongues as the Spirit gave them utterance. The brethren left the room and announced to the governor of Tennessee and the world in general that they would obey God's law, not man's law. A reporter from Chattanooga visited the home of Deacon Ford to learn of the church's decision. He reportedly said, "The law is still on the books in Tennessee where I have my church. We obey Jesus Christ and handle serpents as he commanded."

During a homecoming in 1946 at the old Dolly Pond Church, Sister Minnie Parker, in the anointing of the Lord, took seventeen rattlesnakes out of their boxes and laid them in the floor. She took off her shoes and walked barefoot over them without getting bit. The Bible says in Luke 10:19, "Behold, I give unto you power to tread on serpents and scorpions, and over all the power of the enemy: and nothing shall by any means hurt you." Afterwards, Sister Parker picked up the serpents one by one and put them back into their boxes.

The following spring, the members once again began together at the church in the valley and once again the pastor preached the gospel of Jesus Christ with the signs following the believers. The members shouted and spoke in tongues, and as the anointing moved them, they handled the serpents. Reports of the services soon reached Hamilton County Sheriff Grady Head. On Wednesday, July 23, 1947, the sheriff believed that a service was going to be held at the Dolly Pond Church. The sheriff called in the state police and deputies and led the way to the Dolly Pond Church. There was a large crowd at the church but no service was being held. Pastor Tom Harden arrived and was immediately taken by Sheriff Head, who began questioning him. He asked Harden if he was in charge and Harden responded that he was pastor of the church. Sheriff Head then asked where the serpents were and Pastor Harden told him there were no serpents and, as far as he knew, there was no service scheduled for that night. At that point a reporter interrupted and told Harden, "You might as well be handling serpents tonight. You are going to be arrested sooner or later." Harden told the reporter, "I handle the serpents when the Lord tells me to." After searching the church, the sheriff and other officers left.

The members held their next service on Saturday night. A rattlesnake and copperhead were handled. The following night the police returned to the church by carloads. They found the service going in full swing with more than 100 people present. Unable to find room inside the church, the police looked in the doors and windows. When the police were finally able to get inside the church, they could find no serpents. They left and made their report to Sheriff Head.

Two weeks later two policeman, in plain clothes, Ely and Baker, went to the church at Dolly Pond and took seats in the back of the church. The service began with Tom Harden preaching the gospel of Jesus Christ. He got anointed and started handling serpents. Other members got anointed and handled the serpents, too. When Tom had put the serpents back into the box, the two deputies approached him with their badges showing and identified themselves and placed all the members who had handled the serpents under arrest for violating the state law.

After the policemen had arrested them, the members gathered at the front of the church, praising the Lord for saving their souls from a burning hell. Then they laughed and hugged each other, danced, and sang hallelujah for they were going to jail for the Lord. Tom Harden walked over to one of the policemen and told him that there was no ill feeling and thanked him for the opportunity to suffer for the name of Jesus Christ.

The police had arrested a total of nine people and the car they had come in was too small for all of them. While Baker stayed and kept an eye on the prisoners, Ely drove 5 miles to the nearest phone to call headquarters to send more cars. During the ninety-minute wait the members proceeded with the service (without the serpents) until the police cars arrived to take them away.

The cars arrived at the jail and the members were put into jail cells. Three more members turned themselves into the police the same day. They had to take their families back home. In most cases this meant walking several miles along a lonely road in the darkness. The officers walked along the jail cells, taking down names and addresses so that warrants could be made. A professional bondsman made their bonds, free of charge—this being a sign the members had prayed for. The hearing was one to be long remembered by the people of Hamilton County. They had the hearing in the largest courtroom available. Hundreds of people were there, along with scores of members from the Dolly Pond Church who had come down to give their brethren moral and spiritual support. Although the hearing was set for two in the afternoon many of the members arrived at the courthouse early in the morning.

About thirty minutes before court started, the members formed a ring in the center of the courtroom and started a service—singing and praying, speaking in tongues. Courthouse personnel stopped work and joined in the service. As Judge Goodson entered the courtroom the members became silent and sat down. Their attorney, George Chamlle, and a Chattanooga newspaperman, Fred Hixson, were also there. The hearing was brief, with only the two officers testifying that they had seen the members handling serpents at their church, in violation of the state law. Judge Goodson immediately held all members for grand jury investigation.

After their bonds were made again and they were temporarily free, the members gathered once more for another service which they had on the courthouse steps, directly in front of the jail. Several preachers took turns preaching and all spoke out against the new anti-serpent-handling law. Large crowds of people gathered and traffic was slowed to a near standstill. Before ending the service, members invited everyone to attend their next service and promised some serpents would be handled, "if the Lord was willing."

As I said, the old church in Dolly Pond is gone now, but there is a small new church a few miles down the road from where the old church was. Brother Perry Bettis, the pastor, and his members built the new church. Few know that Dolly Pond still handles as in the old days. No one has died from a bit at the new Dolly Pond Church. It may be tiny, but still it stands firm for God's word. Serpent handling has been going on in Grasshopper Valley and Dolly Pond for three quarters of a century.

Brother Bettis and Rayford Dunn came from Chattanooga, Tennessee, to the Holiness Church of God in Jesus' Name in Newport, Tennessee, for eight days of services. Brother Robert Grooms was the pastor of the church. On June 31, 1981, Perry and Rayford took turns preaching. On Wednesday Brother Perry preached on the fruits of the spirit. He preached from Galatians 5:22 "But the fruit of the Spirit is love, joy, peace, longsuffering, gentleness, goodness, faith." On Saturday, a brother from Virginia preached.

Before homecoming I put a fleece out to the Lord to let me catch a rattlesnake if he wanted me to work in the signs according to Mark 16:18. Fleecing the Lord is to ask for a sign to be sent. I asked the Lord to show me where to find a serpent in three days. I put the fleece out on Wednesday. Wednesday and Thursday went by. On Friday the Lord told me where the rattler was—at the foot of Hall's Top at the old rock wall. My wife Pam and I went up to my folks' house and asked my mom if she wanted to go with to get the serpent. I parked the car beside the rock wall. On the other side of the wall was a tobacco patch. At the end of the patch lay the rattlesnake. It was all coiled up but when it saw me it went into the rock wall in a lightning movement. The Lord told me to go to the road and walk on the other side of the wall. As I walked along the wall, I saw the rattler lying on top of the wall. The Lord told me to get on the wall and get the rattler. The serpent just laid there, so I took a hook and got the rattler, jumped off the wall and put it in the box.

The next day (Saturday) Jesus Christ told me to handle the rattler. I got anointed and got the rattler out of the box and Jesus Christ gave me victory over the serpent. On Sunday, July 8, I took the serpent to the homecoming at the Holiness Church of God in Jesus' Name. At the service the Lord gave John Brown, Rayford Dunn, Perry Bettis, and me the anointing to handle the rattlesnake—a copperhead was also handled. After Perry preached, they had dinner outside on the ground. After dinner we had a second service. Brother Charles Prince came from Canton, North Carolina, and Brother Edward Lee Turner came from Del Rio, Tennessee. About one in the afternoon Brother Prince brought a giant timber rattler and a smaller black rattler and four copperheads. Rayford Dunn got anointed to handle the giant timber rattlesnake and I got anointed to handle a copperhead. After the service Brother Prince gave me a copperhead.

As a result of the law against serpent handling, members that believe in the true gospel of Jesus Christ became very disheartened. The outlook seemed very bleak. But one of their members, Reverend C. D. Morris of LaFollette, Tennessee, was shown the light by the Lord. He sent letters to the pastors of the churches in Tennessee, Virginia, Kentucky, and West Virginia inviting all serpent handlers at the church for the homecoming on Sunday, August 24, 1947. Reverend Morris told them they would have to have order at the service in serpent handling.

Here's the way the Lord told him to conduct services: No member should take a serpent from a box while unbelievers are on the stage; each member must handle the serpent by himself or herself; when done handling, members should place the serpent back in the box; when the anointing moved on someone else they should do the same. The Lord also told Morris that the rules for handling serpents in church would be simple: take the serpents out by the anointing of God, handle the serpent until the anointing starts to leave, put the serpent back in the box. Some people called this the "Morris plan." Morris said if these rules were not followed people would get bitten and maybe even lose their lives. A serpent-handling service under the Morris plan was demonstrated during the day by Oddie Shoupe, Cinda Mays, and Gladys Sturgill, all members of the Church of God in Harlan County, Kentucky. They took turns handling a three-foot-long copperhead as the anointing of the Lord moved on them. Jesus Christ gave great victory that day at the service. The Morris plan worked for his church, but was never adopted by other churches.

In the year 1946, Ulysses Gordon Prince came to Ducktown, Tennessee, preaching the true gospel of Jesus Christ with the signs following. The believers and Prince held a brush harbor meeting 15 miles from Blue Ridge, Georgia, on the edge of the Cherokee National Forest where the Hiawassee River flows on a hill near Stansbury Road. The service got started with a large crowd of people at the service. Prince preached the gospel with the signs following the believers. He reached down to the serpent box and got a rattler out of the box and was handling it when the rattler bit him on the left hand. He became very sick. In those days there were not many cars; people traveled on horseback or walked to church. The members brought up a horse-drawn wagon and laid him in the back. They started for his house—he lived thirty miles away. The road was no good—it was full of potholes and it was so dark that all they could see was the tall Georgia pines and the stars in the sky. Prince said that when the wagon wheel would hit a hole the pain would run all over his body and it felt like he would not see another day. It was almost daylight when they got him home. He got better in about three days. For fourteen years they had serpents in every church service in Ducktown, Tennessee. In 1960, they stopped bringing in serpents because many in the church feared of the law. The last serpent they regularly handled in the Ducktown church was in 1982.

U. G. Prince and his son, Charles, brought serpents back into the service. Charles got anointed to handle the serpent. He went outside to the parking lot, opened the car door, and got the serpent box out. He opened it and reached inside, got the serpents out, and took them into the church. Members that had not handled serpents for twenty-two years took turns handling the serpents. U. G. told Charles to go to the car and get the "deadly thing"—it was *Red Devil* Lye. U. G. got the jar and drank it down in the name of Jesus Christ and several more people also drank the lye. The Bible says in Mark 18, "and if they drink any deadly thing it shall not hurt them." Because of this, serpent handlers can drink deadly poisons when anointed just as Jesus said. All the churches that take up serpents bring the snakes to the services and the "outside" world doesn't know anything about it. If they did, they would call the law. There are many serpent-handling churches that few "outsiders" know about. There was one in Coppertown, Tennessee, The House of Prayer in Jesus' Name. It was started by U. G. Prince in the 1940s.

## Chapter 5

"Neither is their salvation, in any other, for there is none other name under heaven give among men, whereby we must be saved." (Acts 4:12)

# Jesus' Name Handlers in Cocke County, Tennessee

The first time the true gospel of Jesus Christ with the signs following the believers was preached in Cocke County (Del Rio), Tennessee was in 1919 (the same year the first person got bitten in Grasshopper Valley, Tennessee). John Cleming, from Chattanooga, Tennessee, came to Del Rio. He had relatives that lived there. He was also a preacher of the gospel in the Chapel Hollow on the old 15th. The service was held at a Presbyterian church. When John preached the true gospel, he asked the people to catch a rattler and bring it to church the next night and, if the Lord anointed him, he would handle the serpent. The next night no one had brought a snake. Thirty years later a man from Del Rio by the name of McMahan (who lived in Chapel Hollow) went to Big Stone Gap, Virginia, to the Holiness Church of God in Jesus' Name where people were handling serpents. When he returned to Del Rio, he preached the true gospel of Jesus Christ with the signs following the believers. Some of the local people went to a church where they handled serpents. In the same year, 1949, a man came from Virginia to a Brother's house to see if he could find some land to build a serpent-handling church. About a third of a mile from his house, they found some land for sale. He bought it for $75.00 but for some reason the church were not built there. About one mile from Chapel Hollow, McMahan had some land that he donated for the church—approximately 50 by 150 feet. The members built the church that same year. The deed was made to the members of the Church of God in Jesus' Name. It was not until the 1950s that a serpent was brought into the church—the Sand Hill Church in Jesus' Name. McMahan and some brothers from Virginia brought two serpents to the service one night—a rattlesnake and a copperhead. After the service got started, one of the men from Virginia went to the serpent's box and took out the rattler and was handling. it. Brother Ed Ardwood got anointed to handle the copperhead. Frank and two other brothers also handled the snakes. Two men at the church had a warrant taken out on the members that handled the serpents that night. The next day the law rounded up the members and put them in jail. At the hearing, the judge told them he would let them go if they would stop handling serpents and never go to another serpent-handling meeting. But the members told him they were going to obey God, not man. From that time on, serpents have been brought to the services that the Sand Hill Church of God in Jesus' Name. Lester Ranies was pastor of the church at that time.

In the early 1930s the true gospel of Jesus Christ with the signs following the believers was preached in Newport, Tennessee, by Ed Sergeant. Somewhere in Cocke County near Newport there was a small church where the true gospel with the signs following the believers was preached. Ed Sergeant was preaching at that church when an unbeliever brought a rattlesnake that would bite anything that moved. There were a lot of people at that service. As the anointing moved on him, Sergeant opened the serpent's box and grabbed the rattler. It was so huge he had to use both hands to pick it up. As he was handling the rattler it bit him on the hand. It held on to his hand for five minutes as it pumped its venom into Ed Sergeant. People stood there with astonished looks on their faces, wondering what would happen next. Some thought he would fall over dead. It was said there was a doctor at the service and that he said the huge rattler had enough venom to kill ten men. However, Sergeant felt no harm from the venom. He kept handling it in the anointing of God. Jesus Christ gave great victory over the serpent. Ed Sergeant did not get sick nor did he feel any pain—he was a great preacher of the Lord. At that time there were two churches that handled serpents near Newport, Tennessee.

In the early 1950s, another unbeliever named Darus Reed went to the gulf near Grassy Fork in Cocke County to catch a rattler to bring it to the Sand Hill Church of God in Jesus' Name. The following Saturday night, he brought it to the service. Outside, before going in, he told members, "They won't handle this one. I hope it bites the one who takes it up." The service got started and someone brought in Reed's rattler. He was sitting in the back row, hoping the serpent would bite someone. One preacher got up and said he could not handle the rattler but Jesus Christ could. The anointing moved on this preacher and he picked up the rattler and handled it. Fourteen other people handled it, too. Jesus Christ gave a great victory that night.

The first person to get bitten at the Sand Hill Church of God in Jesus' Name was Lester Raines's son, Johnny, in the early 1950s. Some members from Big Stone Gap, Virginia, brought a large rattler to church. Brother Edward Lee Turner said it was the biggest black rattlesnake he had ever seen. It was 6 foot long and 3 inches round. As the service got started Brother Blackburn got anointed and handled the serpent. So did Frank Necessary, McMahan, Lester Raines, and Oscar Pelfery from Virginia. As Lester was handling the serpent, his son Johnny was standing in front of the pulpit. Blackburn got the rattler and laid it around Johnny's neck. The rattler crawled down Johhny's arm and across his left hand. Johnny put his right hand out to get the rattler. It fastened its fangs on his hand. It held on for five minutes as it pumped the venom into the body. Then the rattler fell to the floor. Oscar Pelfery got the serpent and put it in its box. Someone called the law. The church members knew that the law would kill the snakes if they found them so they hid the serpents in the tall weeds in back of the church. The law took some of the members to jail that night. The next day the law came back to the church and got the rattler that bit Johnny. On the way back to Newport, they stopped at Tinman Ball's store. Tinman told me that the rattler was huge and there was venom all inside the box where the serpent had bitten the sides of the box. The law killed the rattler at the courthouse in Newport. Johnny did not die; he got better in about six weeks.

Despite the law, services went on at the church and serpents were handled. Lester Raines became the pastor of the church. Oscar Pelfery and Frank Necessary would come on weekends to hold services. They would catch rattlers in the mountains and bring them to the services. Brother Pelfery would be preaching and would reach down, open the serpent box, and bring out a rattler and handle it in the name of Jesus Christ. Jesus would give perfect victory over the serpents. Brother Pelfrey always told the congregation not to handle the serpents because he handled them, but if God told them to handle them, then to handle the serpents in the anointing of God. A sister said that Blackburn would handle the serpents—he would be preaching and reach down and open the box without looking and bring out the serpents by the handful. Frank Necessary was a big serpent handler. It has been said that two men brought a rattlesnake and wanted to see the serpent handled. They said that Frank got down on his knees and prayed for the Lord to anoint him. The Lord answered his prayer. He opened up the box, got the rattler out, and handled it in the name of Jesus Christ.

In the early 1950s, Edward Lee Turner and his brother were out real early one morning in a field, hauling corn way back up in a hollow. It was cloudy that morning. They were discussing what they had heard a pastor preaching: the signs of the gospel from Mark 16:18—they shall take up serpents. Edward told his brother he thought maybe you could take up the serpents with a hoe handle or a stick. His brother said any sinner could do that. According to Edward Lee, the clouds rolled back on both sides in the sky and a great beam of light broke through the clouds and shone where they were standing. A voice from heaven said, "You have got a handle, use it." They knew the voice was talking about their hands—they should be used to take up serpents. After Johnny Raines had gotten bit, it had put a great fear on Edward Lee—so much so that he said he would never handle serpents.

That same week his brother caught two big copperheads and the following Sunday the church was having a water baptizing service. Brother Oscar Pelfery from Virginia was there. Edward Lee was leading the singing, and at that time, Brother Pelfery got anointed to handle serpents. So Pelfery took the two copperheads out of the box and handled them—Jesus Christ gave him victory over them.

God moved on Edward Lee to take up the serpents. He dropped his songbook and got the serpents and God gave him victory over them. Those were the first serpents Edward Lee had ever handled. Someone turned Edward Lee into the law, so he was arrested and put in jail. That night in jail, while asleep, he dreamed the jailer came to him and asked him if he could handle serpents. Edward Lee told him that he thought he could. The jailer said that he had the biggest black rattlesnake that was caught in Big Stone Gap, Virginia, outside in the courthouse yard. The jailer told him it was the same rattler that had bitten Johnny Raines and it was going to bite him. Edward Lee said that he got up and went with the jailer outside to handle the rattler but he woke up before he got there. At the hearing the judge gave Edward Lee six months on the chain gang for preaching the true gospel of Jesus Christ with the signs following the believers. As he was working on the road, a fellow inmate asked him what he had done and Edward Lee told him. Jesus Christ gave victory to Edward Lee—the judge changed his mind and let Edward Lee go after only three days. Serpent handling went on in the Sand Hill Church until the early 1970s.

That same year at the headquarter church in Big Stone Gap, Virginia, in August, Oscar Pelfery got bitten by a rattler during a service. He died eight hours later. He was a great man of God—he lived by his faith and died for what he believed. Brother Ed

Arwood held the funeral. He said it had 500 people at the service. Some of the congregation from Sand Hill attended the service—they buried Oscar Pelfery August 24, 1968.

After Oscar Pelfrey's death, Bill Myers went to all the churches and told them to stop bringing serpents to the services. The last time serpents were handled at Sand Hill was in the early seventies. Members' fear of being jailed caused the church to split up. The members that still believed in the signs started a new church in Newport, Tennessee.

In August of 1983, I went to see my dad at his house. He lives about a half mile from me. When I arrived there were six sinners talking to dad. They said that they heard there was a rattlesnake up at the old Bell Hill schoolhouse. They said the serpents were in the outbuilding. The Baptist people had held their homecoming at Bell Hill. The sinner's boy was cleaning up the paper plates and cups and putting up the tables they had used for the homecoming. E. H. said, "If you go up there and look for the rattlesnake it will bite you and you will die up there." He was making fun of serpent handling. So my wife, Pamela, and I left to go to Bell Hill. I saw Ricky at Grandma's house, so I stopped and asked him if he would go up to Bell Hill with us to catch a serpent. He got in the car and we left. We arrived at Bell Hill and spent thirty minutes looking for the rattlesnake. There was nothing in the outbuilding, so we started to leave. As we walked toward the car, Jesus Christ spoke to me and said there were two copperheads under some tin where the old Murburn Hall house burned down. We went to the site, I had the serpent box and Pam had the serpent hook. I took the serpent hook and turned the tin over and there lay the biggest copperhead I had seen in these parts. It was 44 inches long and an inch round. I got it with the hook and put it in the box. I turned the other pieces of tin over and found a smaller copperhead. We took the serpents and put them in the car and left. We went to my mom's house (She and my dad were not living together at that time.). My older brother was at work but I talked to my brother, Timothy, then we dropped Ricky off and went back to my dad's house. On the way there, the Lord spoke to me and said that the sinner man was going to stop me and make fun of His word but that He would give me victory over the serpents. When I got to dad's house, the sinner stopped me as the Lord had said. I told them I could not find the rattler but the Lord told me where two copperheads were. E. H. (I do not want to reveal the sinner man's name.) said, "I'd like to see how much you believe in your God." I told him that I knew my God (Jesus Christ). I asked him did he know his god. He and the other sinner men told me they would like to see me handle the serpents that I had just caught. I told them I couldn't handle the serpents but Jesus Christ could. I got the copperheads out of the car and set them in the road. At that time the Lord anointed me to handle the serpents. I opened the box, reached in and got the big copperhead. The anointing was so strong in me that the serpent became like a wet rope. Jesus Christ gave me great victory over the serpent. I handled it in the name of Jesus Christ then put it back in the box. E. H. told me I was a fool for handling serpents. He was making fun of the Word of God. He said, "One thing about it, I won't get bit by a serpent or die by drinking the poison." The Lord spoke to me and I told E. H., "I wouldn't say that. You don't know." Two weeks later he was working at a sawmill and as he reached under some lumber a copperhead bit him on the hand. He went to a doctor for treatment and recuperated. Five months later, he accidentally ate some rat poison at his house. They took him to the hospital and they pumped his stomach and he recovered. Three days later, he came and told me he was sorry for calling me a fool. I hugged his neck and told him I forgave him. One of the other sinners that had been at my dad's house came to my house and told me he had kept in mind what I had told E. H. and it had come to pass, like the Lord said. One thing about it, the Word of God is true and is going to stand. You can talk about me but you had better think twice before you say anything about the Word of God.

On a Monday in July of 1981, I was at a store in Del Rio on Asheville Highway, when a Baptist member of a church on Bull Mountain told me the C brothers had caught a large timberback rattlesnake. They wanted me to go over there. The Lord spoke to me and told me He would give victory over the serpent. My wife and I got there where the C boys live (Again, I do not want to identify sinner boys by name.). As we got out of the car, one of the C boys told me he had the rattler in the barn. As we went in the barn, the serpent started to sing. By the sound of it, it was a large one. When we got to the cage, the rattler looked like a half-bushel tub, all coiled up. It was big and when I saw it the fear came on me. The boy also had a copperhead in the cage and he gave it to me. I got my hook and got the copperhead out of the cage and put it in a box I always carry with me. He said he wanted five dollars for the rattler. I told him I didn't believe in buying serpents. About that time H. C. came in and was looking at me with a funny look on his face. He said he would like to see a Holiness preacher handle the snake without any singing going on. I told him I couldn't handle serpents; it takes the anointing of God to handle the serpents. At that time, the Lord anointed me to handle the serpent and the fear left me. I reached in the cage and got the rattler and handled it in the name of Jesus Christ, then put it back in the cage. One of the C boys reached in to get the serpent out of the cage and the rattler coiled up and struck at him with its mouth open, not missing him by much. He backed up and closed the cage and we left the barn. At that time the C boys were sinners and I guess they thought anyone could handle serpents. I told them we cannot handle serpents; it takes the power of the anointing of God to handle them.

In the summer of 1981, we had a baptizing at the roll hole on the old 15th. They had been preaching the signs for about three months at the Sand Hill Church of God in Jesus' Name. There had not been any serpents at that church for twelve years. The Lord told me to take serpents to the baptizing service and if they started to preach the signs He would give me victory over the rattlesnake. We got to the roll hole about one in the afternoon. The service got started, and Brother Carl and I got in the water and baptized three members of the faith. Brother Carl started to preach the signs of the gospel. The Lord anointed me to get the

rattler. I got out of the water, went to my car, and got the
serpent's box. I opened it up, got the rattler out, and handled it
in the name of Jesus Christ. John Brown, Jr., Carl Parton, Eward
Lee Turner, and Allen Williams also handled the serpents. There
were several people at the service. After the Lord anointed us to
handle the rattler, He told me to put it back in the box, so I did.
We sang and the service came to an end.

The same year, on March 8, Clyde Ricker, Brother Carl, and
Liston Pack baptized his wife and me. The service took place at
the roll hole. The same night, at the Holiness Church of God in
Jesus' Name, Brother Prince got bit by a big, black rattler. He
did not die but was very sick. He recovered three days later.

On Saturday, July 25, 1981, at the Jesus Christ Apostolic
Church at Cosby, Tennessee, some man came from Georgia to
film the service. I took a rattler and copperhead to the service.
Jesus Christ gave Ed Ball and me victory over the serpents during
the service that night. Eight million people by way of television
saw this service.

August 24, 1981, they had a prayer meeting at James David
Martin's house in Del Rio. David had asked me to come to the
service. There were about fifty people there. Adam was holding
the service. David had a copperhead but it was not handled that
night. Adam led the singing, then started preaching. Frank
preached that night, too. The Lord anointed me to preach about
the true church. After the preaching, we had prayers for the sick
and the service ended. The following Saturday night a meeting was
held at Hob's house in Del Rio. I brought the rattler that a
brother had given me in Georgia. The service started at 7:00 with
singing. Adam got up and said that he believed all the Bible and
told everyone to obey the Lord. There was a singer from North
Carolina who performed. I had parked my car across the road at
Jones Chapel—I had left the rattler in my car. David had a
copperhead in his car. As the members were singing, the Lord
told me to go get the serpent and handle it. When I brought the
serpent in to the meeting, I put the box on the ground, opened
it, and got the rattler and started preaching the signs. Adam

jumped up and said he didn't believe in the signs. He got mad and said he was leaving. I told him to stay, that I would leave. I hugged him and told him I loved him, then David, Pam, and I left. We went to Frank Pierce's house to pray for him. After we prayed I told David I was going home. That night I had a dream about Adam—he turned into a big copperhead and seven little copperheads came out of his mouth. I got them and put them in a serpent box. The Lord told me he was a false prophet.

In 1980, I went to Newport and took my copperhead with me. My wife and I stayed in Newport until about 3:30 when we headed back home. We stopped at a store in Del Rio on the Asheville Highway and a sinner man asked me to get my serpent and handle it. I told him I would pray about it and if the Lord said it would be all right I would do it. The Lord told me it would be all right to take the serpent and handle it. A lot of people had gathered at the store. I got the box out of my car and set it on the hood of my car and started to pray. The Lord anointed me to get the copperhead out. I opened the box and told the people to stand back. I reached in and got the serpent and handled it in the name of Jesus Christ. A car passing on the highway came to a complete stop. Jesus Christ gave victory over the serpent and I told them the Bible said they shall take up the serpent. One sinner man said, "That's what the Bible said, I have read it." I put the serpent in the box and put it in the car. Pam and I then went home.

In the 1940s, Hensley preached the true gospel of Jesus Christ with the signs following in the state of North Carolina. The Churches of God that handled serpents were growing throughout the Appalachian Mountains. However they feared officials in Winston-Salem and Durham who made a law banning the practice in 1947. When an interstate conference was held in Durham in 1948, snake handling had already spread all over the Southeast. Even today there is more snake handling being practiced than people think—it is very much alive but mostly underground. If all the believers were to come out of hiding in North Carolina, the churches could not hold them all.

The House of Prayer in Jesus Christ's Name in North Carolina, which was founded in 1970. Reverend John Brown, Sr., is the pastor there now. On August 16, 1981, at their homecoming, Pam and I and her parents arrived at their church around 10:45 A.M. There were a lot of people already there from Kentucky, Georgia, North Carolina, and Tennessee. The service got started at 11:00 with singing and testifying. Someone brought two copperheads to the service but they were not handled. There were prayers for the sick and Brother Perry gave the closing message. After the service there was a picnic dinner, then everyone left for home.

On August 19, 1982, they had another homecoming at that church, with people from four states attending the service. They started the service with singing and testifying for the Lord. Someone brought five serpents. The serpents were handled and Brother Prince drank the deadly thing. I preached that day. Afterward we had a picnic lunch. Jesus Christ gave great victory that day. None of the handlers were bit and Brother Prince was not harmed by the deadly.

The House of Prayer in Jesus' Name that was founded in the early seventies burned down. Brother Marvin Gregg and Brother John Fish built a new church in the early eighties. At the homecoming on June 30, 1985, there were people from West Virginia, Georgia, North Carolina, Tennessee, and Virginia—about 350 people in all. There were fifty serpents at the service. Someone brought strychnine (the deadly thing). Jesus Christ gave victory over all the serpents and some drank the strychnine with victory. Brother Rayford Dunn delivered the message. We had a picnic dinner, then left for home.

In May 3, 1944, members of the Church of God held a service near the village of Stone Creek in a mountainous mining area of southwest Virginia. Oscar Hutton and thirty-five anointed members of the faith were present. During the service, Hutton reach into a wooden box that held a large Eastern Diamondback. Hutton, a preacher of the Church of God, held it up on an open Bible. The believers gathered in a large roped-off area. Two hundred unrepentant sinners surrounded them. They were shown that the serpent's fangs and sacs were intact. Members took up serpents as the anointing moved them. A sister from nearby Kentucky also handled the deadly serpent in the name of Jesus Christ. One member took off his shoes and walked on the diamondback rattler, according to Luke 10:19: "Behold, I give unto you power to tread on serpents." An elderly woman, a member of the faith who was an active serpent handler, said, "I wish the Lord would send us a lion so we could face it." Others said they would like to handle a few cobras. The members of the Church of God also brought out a flaming torch, a mayonnaise jar filled with kerosene, and a homemade wick. Hebrews 11:34 speaking of faith says it "Quenched the violence of fire." The fire was handle in the name of Jesus Christ. No one was burned. A sister of the faith held her face in the flame and was unharmed. One member testimony was that his broken leg was healed by faith in Jesus Christ in twenty-four hours.

Despite several brushes with the law, in thirty-five years since the five signs again become known to the true believers in Tennessee, Virginia, and Kentucky, the Churches of God have increased their membership from a handful to a few thousand. Oscar Hutton preached, "The serpent is a 'devil'; how are you going to conquer a big 'devil' if you can't conquer a little serpent?"

Years ago (1939) in a church service in Kentucky, this took place. Aurthur was going to a church service after he got off from work. He asked Oscar Hutton if he had any serpents. Oscar said no. He said Aurthur asked if he would be at the service tonight. He said that he would if he did not have to work overtime. Hutton got off from work and did not have to work that following evening. When he got home, a sinner man brought a big rattlesnake to Hutton. Oscar Hutton got anointed to handle it. He opened the sack and poured it on the ground. He reached out and got it with his right hand. He handled the rattlesnake in the name of Jesus Christ. He then put it in a box that he had at his house. About six o'clock, he left for the church. When he got there he went in through a side door. The pastor of the church had never seen the serpents handled and did not fully understand the signs of the gospel. Hutton walk in with the serpent box and set it on the pulpit. Hutton walked back to the wall and stood by Brother Aurther. The anointing moved on Hutton. He walked back and forth across the floor. He then opened the serpent box and went back and stood against the wall. Auther got anointed to go get the serpent. The house was full of people. Someone hollered at Aurther, "Will the serpent bite?" This got Aurther's mind off of the Lord. At that time the Lord anointed Oscar Hutton and he went to the pulpit where the serpent box was. He reached in and got the serpent out. He handled it in the name of Jesus Christ. Then the pastor of the church got anointed. He took the serpent from Hutton and walked back and forth in front of the church praising the Lord. After the service was over, he told the members of the church that the signs of the gospel are true and for us today just as they have always been true.

This is the history of the Jesus' Name handlers. We know the signs of the gospel to be true, and just as the disciples did, we confirm the word with signs following. In Mark:16:20 the Bible says, "And they went fourth, and prached everywhere, the Lord working with them and confirnming the word with signs following." This means they handled serpents back then even as we do today. Serpent handling is a sign to the believers; if you are a true believer in the Word of God, these signs will follow you. You don't have to go in the mountains to catch a serpent; the unbelievers will bring them to you. Once I was praying and asking God for greater revelation on serpent handling. Within two weeks two men came to the house where I lived with a rattlesnake in a sack. They had caught it that day in Hartford at place back in the hollow called Mill Creek. They asked me if I could handle it. I said, "No, it takes the power of Jesus Christ to handle serpents." The Lord told me to get the sack. I got it. I told the men to step back. I opened the sack and poured the rattle on the ground. Jesus Christ gave me victory over the rattler. I put him back in the sack. The two man ask if I wanted to buy the serpent; I told them no. The signs of the gospel will follow the believers. You don't have to buy serpents. Jesus Christ will send the serpents to be handled. I have always prayed to Jesus Christ to tell me where to find serpents. If he tells me where they are, all I have to do is get in the car and go to the place where he told me, and the serpent is always there. If Jesus Christ tells me not to go, I won't. We get into very deep trouble when we do not obey the Lord. Jesus Christ knows all things; he knows the time and place for everything.

"If they drink any deadly thing" does not mean go and buy poison and drink it. In the Middle Ages, many of the authorities were having trouble with the followers of Christ. They tried to poison those who believed the Gospel of Christ, but the poison failed to do its work and did not kill them. The fourth sign, "if they drink any deadly thing," means Christians were killed, by many kinds of deaths—by burning them, by feeding them to lions—that if you are preaching the gospel of Christ, and some unbelievers try to kill you with poison, it will not hurt you.

## Chapter 6

"For now I am ready to be offered, ands the time of my departure is at hand." (2 Timothy 4:6)

# Jesus' Name Handlers in Newport, Tennessee

Reverends Jimmy Ray Williams, Walter Newcome, Alfred Ball, and Liston Pack founded the Holiness Church of God in Jesus' Name at Newport, Tennessee, in the early spring of 1969. It was near Carson Spring Community on the old Sevierville Highway. They converted a remote hunting lodge into a church for a year. The members paid fifteen dollars a month for the building and finally in early 1970 the members bought the land and building for $1000. The deed was made to the members of the Holiness Church of God in Jesus' Name.

In the early 1970s, I talked to Reverend Williams in the early seventies about his church. "We believe our church is the closest to the original apostles' doctrine than any other churches," said Reverend Jimmy Williams, who had been pastor of the church for two years. Reverend Williams, a native of Cocke County, was married and had three children. He had been in the Holiness Church of God in Jesus' Name for five years. "I was formerly a member of the original Church of God," he said, "but then I heard about a church in Big Stone Gap, Virginia, that went deeper into the Scriptures." The last phrase means to taking every word in the 1611 King James' version of the Bible literally. This includes Luke 10:19. "Behold, I give unto you power to tread on serpents and scorpions, and over all the power of the enemy: and nothing shall by any means hurt you." "There is no skill to handling serpents," says Reverend Williams, "and there is no special way to keep the serpents from biting you. It is no test, it does, however, require a certain amount of faith." Certainly, there is danger involved in handling a rattlesnake or copperhead and Reverend Williams agrees. "Four people were bitten this summer," he said, "but none went to the doctor and they're all in good health. We don't have anything against doctors, it's just a matter of who you're putting your trust in." Reverend Williams also readily agrees that his religion or church is often misunderstood. The name of Jesus Christ has caused confusion to many. Reverend Williams said, "We believe only in Him." "The Father, the Son, and the Holy Ghost are only *names* for Jesus Christ. Because of the name of Jesus Christ, worldly friends turn against you and accuse you of being a madman."

The church baptizes its members by immersion in the nearby French Broad River. The church has at least one baptism a month throughout the winter and summer. The church has an enrollment of 50, but as many as 200 have attended some services. Reverend Williams says, "Many people who come don't participate in the serpent handling. We don't force anyone to handle them. Some people think we put serpents on people but we never do that. When a member is ready to handle a serpent, he knows it. Snake handling is against the law in some states, but our church is doing nothing against the law. The law says it's a crime to display snakes to endanger a person's life, such as putting a serpent on someone. We don't do that. The Holiness Church of God in Jesus' Name holds services Saturday, Sunday, and Wednesday nights. We do nothing secret here. Everyone is welcome to come."

Jimmy Williams was a great man of God. He believed in the world of God; he has been lawed for the Word of God. He has been in jail for the name of Jesus Christ and some of his best friends have turned against him. Before his death in the signs in 1973, he wrote about how he wanted to be remembered. He wrote that upon his death his funeral should be conducted at the church by the elders of the church. He wanted "Precious Memories" to be sung and "Why Not Tonight." He wanted the

cheapest casket for his funeral. He wanted them to open the
Bible to Mark 16:18, to take up serpents, and to drink poison. He
wanted his body put on the hill from the church; he wanted them
to read 2 Timothy 4:6–8: "For I am now ready to be offered, and
the time of my departure is at hand. I have fought a good fight, I
have finished my course, I have kept the faith: Henceforth there
is laid up for me a crown of righteousness, which the Lord, the
righteous judge, shall give me at that day: and not to me only, but
unto all them also that love his appearing." He wanted the elders
to show people that God's ways are right and man's ways are
wrong. He didn't want any neckties and he wanted the brothers
that handled serpents as pallbearers.

Jimmy Ray Williams was a great man of God. The only time
he was bitten by a snake was one night in a service at the
Holiness Church of God in Jesus' Name. There was a woman who
went to the serpent box that had a copperhead in it. The
copperhead jumped out of the box at the woman. Jimmy was not
anointed to handle the serpent. He got the serpent so the woman
would not get bitten. The copperhead bit Jimmy on the right
hand. He did not go to a doctor and he got better in three days.
Reverend Williams had been lawed several times for the gospel of
Jesus Christ—in the state of Tennessee two times and also the
state of Virginia for serpent handling. Jimmy said he would never
back up from the Word of God. He endured to the end for the
gospel of Jesus Christ that he loved. Jesus Christ gave His life on
a cross and died for our sins. Jimmy Ray Williams gave his life for
the gospel. He went to rest in the year 1973 and had hope for
resurrection at the second coming of Jesus Christ. In 1
Thessalonians 4:16 it says, "For the Lord himself shall descend
from heaven with a shout, with the voice of the archangel, and
with the trump of God, and the dead in Christ shall rise first."

On July 8, 1979, at the Holiness Church of God in Jesus'
Name at Newport, Tennessee, Brother Carl Parton was pastor at
that time. It was a Sunday service and the church was packed with
people. There were people from Georgia, Carl Porter, Jr., and his
family, another couple from Jolo, West Virginia, Pam and me,

John and Mary Fish, Gene Shurbert and family, Rayford Dunn
and Perry Bettis from Chattanooga, Tennessee, Clyde Ricker
from Hot Springs, North Carolina, and many more. They had
singing and shouting and testimony. They had about eighteen
serpents. Clyde Ricker got anointed and handled three or four
rattlesnakes. They had some strychnine in a jar but no one drank
any at the homecoming that day. Brother Parton preached from
Matthew 25: "Then shall the kingdom of heaven be likened unto
ten virgins, which took their lamps, went forth to meet the
bridegroom. And five of them were wise, and five were foolish.
They that were foolish took their lamps, and took no oil with
them: But the wise took oil in their vessels with their lamps.
While the bridegroom tarried, they all slumbered and slept. And
at midnight there was a cry made, 'Behold, the bridegroom
cometh; go ye out to meet him.' Then all those virgins arose, and
trimmed their lamps. And the foolish said unto the wise, 'Give us
of your oil; for our lamps are gone out.' But the wise answered,
saying, 'Not so, lest there be not enough for us and you: but go ye
rather to them that sell, and buy for yourselves.' And while they
went to buy, the bridegroom came, and they that were ready went
in with him to the marriage: and the door was shut. Afterward
came also the other virgins, saying, 'Lord, Lord, open to us.' But
he answered and said, 'Verily I say unto you, I know you not.
Watch therefore, for ye know neither the day nor the hour
wherein the Son of man cometh.'"

After the service, we had a picnic dinner and some people
left for home. Junior Porter and I were looking at the serpents in
the church and Jesus anointed me to handle a copperhead and a
rattler. Glenn Dukes also handled a rattler. Pam and I left soon
after that. We had a real good meeting that day. Jesus gave us a
great victory.

Brother Carl Parton came into the faith or the Holiness
Church of God in Jesus' Name in 1974 or 1975. He was the
assistant pastor at Bat Harbor Log Church. The members of the
Holiness Church asked him if he would hold two weeks of service
at their church. When he did he became a member and was

ordained by the church and he and his family was baptized according to Acts 2:38. He also preached in other Churches of the Lord Jesus Christ all over Tennessee and Georgia. It was at the Full Gospel Church of Jesus Christ, early in 1983, that I last heard him preach. He preached out of Matthew 24. It was the best sermon I ever heard preached.

On a Sunday, July 8, 1980, the Holiness Church of God in Jesus' Name held their fourth annual homecoming service. The congregation included about thirty men, women, and children. I brought a rattlesnake and copperhead with me. The members at this church continue to handle serpents at their religious services. The service that day began like those at many small fundamentalist, country churches with singing, prayer and testimonies of their faith. Six men seated next to the pulpit got anointed by the power of God and were dancing and speaking in tongues as the anointing moved them. At this time, one man, anointed by the Holy Ghost of God reached his hand into the serpent box and pulled out a large timber rattler. Rayford Dunn said that God had given power over the devil. He shouted, gripping the serpent near its tail and the middle while pointing its head from himself. Walking around the pulpit, he rested the serpent's head in the open palm of his hand while clutching its body with the other hand. Its tongue darted at the surrounding group of men and its yellow belly twisted violently to escape the man's grip but the serpent never once showed its fangs. The serpents were passed to other members—John Brown, Clyde Ricker, and me—who took turns hugging and swinging the serpents. At times we would press its head against our bodies. Sometimes we would bring its gray head close to our own sweating faces to capture its eyes in a challenging glare. Suddenly the serpent was put back in the box, only to be brought out again later when someone else felt the anointing of the Lord. A smaller copperhead was also handled. Jesus Christ gave great victory that day.

On the second Saturday night in November of 1984, at the Holiness Church of God in Jesus' Name, the service got started.

The church was full that night. The sisters went to the prayer room to pray. After prayer they came back to their seats. Henry Pack and Brother Prince went to the prayer room to pray before the preaching began. Henry walked from the prayer room with his hands held high over his head, praising the Lord. There were four boxes of serpents that night. Brother Charles Prince and Grady Henry (from North Carolina) had brought a couple of boxes that held cottonmouths and one box that held a large eastern diamondback that was 5 feet long with a head as big as a man's fist. It had a set of rattles 4 inches long. Liston Pack opened the service and told the congregation to obey the Lord. If they felt the anointing to take up the serpents. At that time the singing started with "Roll Me Over The Tide." Once the music began, Brother Henry got anointed and danced across in front of the pulpit and straight to the serpent boxes. He opened the box that held four cottonmouths and two rattlers. He reached in his hand and brought out all six snakes in the name of Jesus Christ. As Henry held the serpents close to his chest and let them crawl around his arm, Prince got anointed by the Lord. He bounded on one foot across the room with the first finger on his right hand held high. As the large rattler was brought out of the box, Brother Prince was praising the Lord and handling the serpent. He let its head come before his and smiled. As he danced with it, I was praying for the brothers handling the serpents. As the anointing moved on me, I rose and joined the circle of the anointed. Prince handed me the canebrake rattler and I handled the serpent in the name of the Lord. Prince danced outside the circle towards the serpent boxes and grabbed the gigantic rattler. The big serpent waved back and forth in his hand, rattling a deadly warning. At this time, Prince took the canebrake rattler from me and lay it on the floor of the church, he took off his shoes and walked on the serpents in the name of Jesus Christ, according to Luke 10:19. He stepped on the midsection of the serpent with his right foot pressing with the full weight of his body on it. Prince began to shout praises to the Lord. He took the diamondback from around his neck and began to dance on one foot, holding the serpent high and praising the Lord. Two jars of strychnine were on either side of the pulpit. One jar was filled to the brim and the other jar was a little under half full with its crystal clear, deadly liquid. After the serpents were put back in the boxes, Prince walked behind the pulpit and took a drink of strychnine. Then the anointing moved on him to handle fire, so he picked up a torch filled with flammable liquid. Someone lit the wick and the flame was over a foot high and he held the orange and blue flame under the chin while walking back and forth in front of the pulpit and preached the Word of God. Prince said the serpents do not have the keys to heaven or hell. Jesus Christ knows we are not looking to die; we are looking for eternal life. There was sweat pouring from his face, but he did not get burned. Minutes later Prince took several drinks of strychnine from both jars and said in the name of Jesus Christ it would not hurt him.

Liston Pack then began to preach. He said the church was no different from other fundamentalist religions and that he had been witness to great wisdom and knowledge and prophecy at the church. The Bible says you should know the truth and it will set you free. It takes faith to please God. The way you know you have the spirit of God is if you love one another. Education is great, but without the spirit of the Lord, you are nothing. At the end of the sermon an old lady in a white dress, her hair was gray with age, walked to the front of the church, arms outstretched in the ancient prayer stance. Prince, Pack, Grooms, and I laid our hands on top of her head and began to pray diligently for her. A film crew from East Tennessee State University and students from Wake Forest College in Winston-Salem, North Carolina (The film crew was headed by Tom Burton, a professor of English, and Tom Headley, associate professor in Communications who have produced this.) recorded this documentary on the Holiness Church of God in Jesus' Name.

Brother Prince's faith in Jesus Christ was strong. He believed as Paul wrote—the last enemy that shall be defeated is death. In the years that he has been a handling serpent, he had found peace within himself and with Jesus Christ. In the end there was no fear in him—he walked on serpents, drank strychnine, and handled fire in the name of Jesus Christ. Prince grew up in the church. His father is the pastor near Rome, Georgia. He moved to Canton, North Carolina, where he repented in 1977, and started to obey the signs of the gospel in late 1979. The first time he handled a serpent in the church was in the early eighties in Marshal North Carolina, at the House of Prayer in the Name of Jesus Christ. The first time he drank lye was at his house in Canton, North Carolina. He went home to his bedroom and put two tablespoons of lye in a pint jar of water. He got in the closet and closed the door. He prayed to the Lord to anoint him after he prayed for hours. Then he got the jar of lye and drank it down. It set his insides on fire. According to Prince, "From my lips to the bottom of my stomach was burning. I heard a voice tell me that it would do no good to go to bed, I was going to die. The voice told me it would do no good for me to go to church, I was going to die. I knew it was the devil talking to me. I laid down on my bed and opened my Bible to Mark 16:18 and when I read that verse the fire went out." Prince traveled hundreds of miles throughout East Tennessee, North Carolina, West Virginia, Virginia, Georgia, Kentucky, Mexico, and South America to preach the true gospel of Jesus Christ with the signs following the believers.

On Sunday, July 7, 1985, the Reverend Charles Prince was having a church service. Several people came from other states to attend the service. Before the service got started the law of Heywood County had a disagreement over which the higher of laws was—that of God or the law of the land. The Sheriff took four boxes of poisonous snakes from the service and the service went ahead as scheduled. They had singing—a group from Tennessee was there with an electric guitar and an organ. The congregation also had part in the singing with clapping, dancing, singing, and playing the cymbals. As the anointing moved on the people, they would handle fire in the name of Jesus Christ. Some of the anointed would hold a flame from an acetylene torch to their hands and not get burned. Prince told them the Bible says faith quenches the violence of fire—it doesn't put the fire out, just relieves the pain. During the service, the members said that the sheriff's department should not interfere in a service. Prince told the sheriff's department that they were interfering with the Word of the Lord. Later on in the service a young man was anointed by the power of God, went to his car, a black Ford Escort, opened the car door, and opened a serpent box. He reached in and brought out a cottonmouth and was handling it in the name of Jesus Christ. He walked through the crowd with the serpent in his hand. When he got to the tent, the anointed passed the serpent to one another in front of the tent. Charles Prince was handling the serpent when two deputies ran to Prince and got him while he still had the serpent in his hand. The deputies took Prince behind a patrol car where he was ordered to drop the serpent. Deputy pulled his gun and started firing at the serpent. He shot at it five times, hitting the cottonmouth once and killing it.

Prince, Williams, and Wiley Belcher of Walland, Tennessee, were taken aside by the deputies for questioning. They were told that if the serpents were found to be poisonous they would be charged with serpent handling, which violates a state law. Jesus Christ says in Luke 21:12: "But before all these, they shall lay their hands on you, and persecuting you, delivering you up to the synagogues, and into prisons, being brought before kings and rulers for my name's sake." John Brown preached the true gospel of Jesus Christ with the signs following the believers to a crowd of 300 people. Later on in the service, a man came up to the tent saying he wanted to repent and to become a Christian. He stood with crossed arms as Prince and several other members gathered around him, praying aloud. Prince told them, "We have a chance to tell a lot of people about Jesus Christ."

Serpents taken from the religious service in Canton were determined to be poisonous on Thursday by an official of the North Carolina Museum of Natural History. They were all venomous. Curator J. P. took ten serpents—two cottonmouths, three copperheads, and five rattlesnakes.

A serpent is determined poisonous if the glands of venom are still attached to its mouth. Looking at a serpent, you can tell if the glands have been removed. It's not necessary to pry the mouth of the serpent open. If someone takes the fangs off a serpent, trying to prevent it from biting, the fangs will grow back. The handling of poisonous serpents is a misdemeanor in North Carolina with a fine and punishable up to $500 or six months in jail. The serpent was to be used in the church service to confirm the gospel of Jesus Christ. At the service that Prince was holding in Canton, North Carolina, no arrests could be made until the sheriff's department received an official report and send it to the district attorney.

On Sunday, August 4, 1985, Pamela and I left Del Rio and went to Hartford at Key's Store to meet Allen Williams and go to the service in Canton that Prince was holding. Allen got there at 10:45. We parked our car at Key's store and got into Allen's car. It took about an hour to drive to the service. Allen had a large yellow rattler that Prince had told him to bring to the service. When we arrived, several people from other states were there. The deputies of Heywood County were driving up and down the road. Prince had a table fixed under the tent to put the serpents. There were already two large rattlers, two smaller rattlers, and six copperheads. The deputies stopped at the service about noon with sticks in their hands. The Lord told me to go and shake their hands and to hug their necks and make them welcome. Jimmy Williams and I did as the Lord directed. The deputies just hung their head and, about that time, Sheriff arrived. Charles was waiting for his father to arrive from Georgia—he was going to preach that day. He, his wife, and his daughter Ann and her husband finally arrived. The service got started and the churches from Greenville, Marshall, Newport, and Morristown were there to help with the service. There would have been more, but the sheriff told the people that were parked near the road to get in their cars and go. If they didn't, he was going to get the county to

move them, so several people left. Prince got anointed to sing a
song, so he got a torch and lit it and was handling the fire in the
name of Jesus Christ. Flames licked at Prince's neck and face as
he danced with the homemade torch. It did not burn him. He
also put his hand in the flames several times. "The Lord has been
good to me," Prince told the crowd. "The Bible is true. I don't
care if there's a law or there isn't a law." Prince then asked his
dad to come and preach. Ulysses Gordon Prince—he preached
the gospel of Jesus Christ with the signs following the believers.
Several times during the service, Ulysses Gordon told the crowd,
"This isn't a serpent show, this is not a ballgame, this is not a get
together. This is an old-time, Holy Ghost service. I have never
been arrested for nothing but preaching the Word of God."
During the sermon, the Sheriff had Allen Williams arrested and
charged with serpent handling. Two deputies got Allen by the
arm and took him to their car and took him to the Heywood
County Jail. As Ulysses Gordon was preaching on the five signs,
Charles pulled a number of serpents from a table drawer and
began to handle them in the name of Jesus Christ. The Sheriff
immediately ran to Prince, trying to enforce the manmade law.
He told Prince to drop the serpents and to drop them now.
Prince was backing off from the sheriff and the sheriff ran up to
Prince and grabbed the rattler and pulled it from Prince's hand.
The sheriff tried to throw it down but his hand would not open.
Its head was coming to his hand and its mouth was open. The
sheriff had fear on him—I will never forget the look on his face
as the serpent's fangs sank deep in the flesh of his hand and blood
was running down his hand. Immediately his hand opened and the
serpent dropped to the ground. He tried to kill the snake with
the stick he had in his other hand but failed. One of the deputies
got his foot on the serpent and stood there, the sheriff walked to
a nearby state highway patrol car and told the officer that a rattler
had bitten him. He was taken to the hospital.

"He asked for it," preached Ulysses Gordon Prince. "That's
what happens when you try to stop the gospel. He's got no

business interfering with God's work. He can't blame anyone but himself."

About five minutes before the sheriff was bitten, John Fish, from White Pine, Tennessee, arrived at the service. The Lord had woke him up and told him that some of the members were going to jail. Allen was already in jail by the time he got there. After the sheriff was bitten, they got Prince and took him to jail. So the rest of us cleaned up the tent and got the rattler the deputy had been standing on and put in a box. Most of the people had already gone. Pamela rode to the courthouse with Linda, Prince's wife. I went to jail with John Fish. Allen was already out of jail. Prince paid his bond; he was released on a $200 bond for handling serpents during the July 7 service. Charles Prince, aged forty-seven, of Canton, North Carolina, was charged with handling reptiles of a poisonous nature and obstructing officers, according to the Heywood County Sheriff's Department. Prince was released on a $700 bond soon after the service. Prince was still wearing a light blue shirt blackened by the smoke while he held flaming kerosene under his chin during the service. When he was released from jail he said of the snake biting, the sheriff, "This proves the Bible is right. Jesus Christ said we would be persecuted. The mark of the beast is coming. Even so, we are going to put God first."

The local newspaper gave an account of the snakebite incident. It said that Haywood county sheriff Jack Arrington, appearing fit but nursing a rash on his hand arm caused by medication, made his first public appearance this morning. It said a deadly canebrake rattlesnake bit him on Sunday, August 4, 1985. Arrington was quoted as saying, "I feel pretty good but the irritation from the rash keeps me from sleeping." Arrrington said he was still tired.

The paper went on to say that Arrington was released from Haywood county hospital Monday morning. He was bitten on the hand while trying to break up a snake-handling religious service. Arrington was quoted as saying, "I want to thank the folks for what they have done for me and the nurses and doctors at the

hospital that took care of me." Arrington added that he would
return to work whenever the doctors told him to.

During the hastily called press conference in his office,
Arrington recounted the series of events that led up to his being
bitten and his reaction after being bit. Arrington said he was
standing along the perimeter of the service waiting for someone
to go to one of the cars to get the snakes, as they had done at a
pervious service July 7, 1985. Arrington said that as he stood
watching he saw a flourish of activity on the other side of the
tent. Arrington said he raced through the tent and got alongside
Charles Prince, the Canton man who conducted the service.
Arrington said his grabbing of the snake was not premeditated.
When he swung around, he grabbed the snake about 6 inches
below its head. Arrington said it was an instant reflex reaction.
He then wrestled with the snake. He was trying to get a better
grip on the snake when it bit him. Arrington said he threw the
snake on the ground after he was bitten and put his foot on it to
keep it from getting out into the crowd at that point. "I didn't
want to just drop it and let it get out among the people," he said.
When asked what was going through his mind immediately after
he was bitten, Arrington said he was going to get treatment right
away.

On August 28, 1985, Allen Williams, aged twenty, of
Newport, Tennessee, pleaded guilty to the judge on one count of
handling reptiles of a poisonous nature at Canton, North
Carolina. This was heard by a judge in district criminal court in
Heywood County. Williams was sentenced to thirty days in jail.
This sentence was suspended and he was placed on one year
probation. He was also fined $100. Brother Charles Prince could
have faced up to eighteen months in prison, but before he had
his hearing before the judge the Lord took him home to be with
Him.

# Chapter 7

"Yea, though I walk through the Valley of the shadow of death I shall fear no evil, for thou art with me." (Psalm 23)

## The Death of Charles Prince in Greensville, Tennessee

At the Apostolic Church of God of the Lord Jesus in Greeneville, Tennessee, the service started at about 7:30 in the evening. The pastor was holding a three-day meeting before the homecoming on Sunday, August 18, 1985. A brother from Jolo, West Virginia, brought the yellow rattler that had bitten Prince the month before. There were several people from other states at the service that night. The service started with singing. During the singing, Brother Prince brought in a black rattler. He had also brought strychnine with him, but he left it in the car because there was strychnine already at the service. Prince went to the serpent box and got the yellow rattler (He already had the black rattler.). He was handling the serpents while, at the same time, trying to light a torch. He tried three times but the torch kept going out. He laid the rattlers on his left arm and the rattlers' heads were next to his left hand. That was when the yellow rattler bit him, then the black one, with a lightning movement, bit Prince four times. This happened about 8:30. The serpents were put back in their boxes. Two more brothers drank some strychnine from the jar on the pulpit. Prince got the torch again and this time he succeeded in lighting it and handled the fire for a long time. He also drank from the jar of strychnine three times.

He seemed to be all right. After about an hour and a half the serpents' venom started to take hold. He started to have pain; his arm and hand was swollen and he got sick. The brothers and sisters started praying for him. He kept getting worse. Someone suggested they should get him to someone's house. Brother Reed said they could take Prince to his house in Limestone, Greene County, Tennessee. After they got Prince to the Reed's house he told them that whatever happened, he didn't want to go to the hospital. He made it plain to his wife, Linda, if he became unconscious not to take him to the hospital. His trust was in God and if God wanted him to go, he would go. This was Saturday, August 17. I was not at the service when he got bitten. I was in North Carolina, preaching at the House of Prayer in the Name of Jesus Christ.

The next day, Sunday, August 18, I went to the Homecoming at the Apostolic Church of God in Greeneville, Tennessee. First, I went to Newport and picked up Pam's parents, John and Bonnie Ford, to go with us. We got to the church about 10:30 A.M. but no one was there. About 10:45 Brother Marvin Gregg's boy and girl came to the church. The girl got out of their car and told us that Brother Prince had gotten bit by the rattlers the night before and that their father was over at the Reed's house and had been there all night with Brother Prince. People started to arrive for the service from other states (Kentucky, Virginia, West Virginia, and North Carolina). The pastor arrived at the church about noon and the service got started. The service started with singing and then some brother from Kentucky went to the serpent box and took the rattler up and began to handle it. Several other brothers and I got anointed to handle the serpents. Some woman got two rattlers and was walking back and forth in front of the church. Brother Raymond, from Kentucky, got the strychnine and drank from the pint jar. Brother Terry also drank some strychnine. Then the preacher, Cory, started the sermon. Jesus Christ gave victory that day at the service. Afterwards, we had a picnic dinner. After dinner Pam and I followed John Fish to

Limestone, Tennessee. We got there a little after two in the morning.

We parked the car about 300 feet from the house. As we entered the house, we could hear people praying for Brother Prince. I went into the room where Brother Prince was resting. His left arm was swollen twice his size. His fingers were swollen so badly that he could not bend them. He looked up at me with a smiling face. He said he was in great pain and then asked me to kneel down beside him and pray for him. His family from Rome, Georgia, was in the room with him. His sister, Ann, was holding ice on his hand. They left to get something to eat. I stayed with him and prayed and held ice on his hand. Other members started coming into the room to pray for him. About an hour and a half later, his sister came back. Prince asked for some tea and, as he drank it, he asked his sister to recite the 23rd Psalm:

The Lord is my Shepherd, I shall not want
He maketh me to lie down in green pastures,
He leadeth me beside the still waters,
He restoreth my soul,
He leadeth me in the path of righteousness for His
    Name's sake.
Yea, though I walk through the Valley of the shadow of
    death
I shall fear no evil, for Thou art with me
Thy rod and Thy staff, they comfort me
Thou preparest a table before me, in the presence of
    mine enemies
Thou anoinest my head with oil
My cup runneth over
Surely goodness and mercy shall follow me all the days
    of my life
And I will dwell in the House of the Lord forever.

When he requested that, I knew that Brother Prince was going home to be with the Lord. About 5:30 P.M., we went back to Newport to take Pam's parents home.

On Monday morning, about 7:30, his head in the hands of John Brown, Sr., Prince's last words were, "The angel is coming to take me home. I believe I can rest now." With that, he closed his eyes and turned over and went to sleep in Jesus Christ and he quit breathing. Thirty-six hours after he was bitten (five times on the left hand), Prince went home to be with the Lord, Monday morning, 7:30 A.M., August 17, 1985.

On Thursday, August 22, 1985, the funeral service for Charles H. Prince was held at the Mt. Carmel House of Prayer in Jesus' Name at Ducktown, Tennessee, (about 15 miles from Blue Ridge, Georgia). The hearse arrived at the church about 11:30 in the morning. The funeral director backed the hearse up to the front of the church. One man opened the door of the hearse and the six pallbearers got the casket (which was silver) and carried it to the front of the church. U.G. Prince, Charles' father, held the funeral service. He started the service with a tape that he had recorded in Canton, North Carolina, on Sunday, August 4, 1985—the day the sheriff of Heywood County got bitten by the large rattler.

After the sheriff had taken the serpents from Charles, the tape had Charles singing "I Am a Holiness Man." After he played the tape, Ulysses Gordon quoted scriptures from St. John: "Jesus wept." Ulysses Gordon preached some and then he asked Terry Morgan to sing Charles' favorite song, "The Master Plan." Two more men got up to sing then Ulysses Gordon had John Brown, Rayford Dunn, Glen Dukes, Charles Cory, Tommy Coots, and me testify and sing two songs. Gene Shurbert and two other pastors I didn't know testified. Then Charles's sister Ann got up, testified and sang two songs. U. G. then turned the service over to the funeral director.

One of the funeral assistants opened the casket and the director asked the people to come up and pay their last respects. There were about 400 people at the service and the service had been unpublicized. If it had been publicized, I feel certain there would have been more than a thousand people there. There were people from five states. After the members had paid their last respects the funeral director closed the casket. The pallbearers carried the casket back to the hearse. They drove across the road from the church. Ulysses Gordon Prince asked Brothers Cory and Shurbert to hold the graveside service. After the preaching Brother Marvin Gregg testified and sang. After this they prayed as they lowered the casket into the grave. They covered the casket slowly with dirt. In the year 1945, Charles's father, U. G. Prince, held his first serpent-handling service where they buried Charles thirty-nine years later in 1985. Brother Charles H. Prince was laid to rest in the Mt. Carmel Cemetery at two in the afternoon, Thursday, August 22, 1985.

# Chapter 8

"He that findeth his life shall lose it: and he that loseth his life for my sake shall find it." (Matthew 10:39)

# The Death by Serpent Bite of George Hensley and Other Jesus' Name Believers

Nobody knows for sure how many people have died practicing the signs. Most people try to tally deaths by newspaper accounts. Here are some of the deaths that I know about.

The first death in the signs was in a church in Kentucky during the early 1940s. The name of the member is unknown.

The second person that died in the signs was an unknown man who got bitten in Kentucky and was taken back to Tennessee where he died twelve hours later.

The first person bitten in Tennessee was Lewis Ford. He was bitten by a rattler in a service in Daisy, Tennessee, and died seventy minutes later. This death was in 1945.

Next year, 1946, Clint Jackson got bitten in service near Daisy, Tennessee, by a rattler and died forty-five minutes later.

In 1945, in LaFollette, Tennessee, Johnny Hensley got bitten by a rattler during a service and died seconds later.

An unknown woman got bitten during a service somewhere in Tennessee and died.

Lee Valentine, who had been bitten hundreds of times, was bitten during a service in Alabama and died. Two more unknown men got bitten in Kentucky and died.

In 1955, in Florida, George Hensley, aged seventy-eight, who had been bitten hundreds of times before, was bitten and died.

His death by serpent bite ended the career of the most notorious and well known of the early serpent handlers.

George Hensley's last service was on a warm summer day in Atha, Florida, at a place called Lester's Flat. The sky was clear and blue that day. Hensley had preached the gospel of Jesus Christ with the signs following the believers for forty-five years. He had preached in West Virginia, Georgia, Kentucky, Tennessee, North Carolina, South Carolina, Virginia, and Florida. It is said that he had suffered 447 serpent bites and never had any medical attention. He believed that if you got bit by a serpent during a service and you died, then it was your time to go. He once said, "If you get bitten a thousand times, if the Lord don't want you to die, you won't." He believed if the gospel was good enough to live by, it was good enough to die by. He laid down his life for what he believed and for the gospel of Jesus Christ. He never backed down from the gospel. He believed in every word in the Bible. During the forties, at a service in Kentucky, he was bitten on the face by a large yellow rattlesnake. As the rattler brought its head back from his face, one of its fangs broke off in his nose. Blood was running down his face, but the Lord spoke to Hensley and told him he was not going to die. His head was swollen to twice its size and his neck was swollen so big that he had to sit on the side of his bed and hold his hands to both sides of his neck so he could breathe. For three days he suffered, then he recovered. At the next service he attended, he got a rattlesnake and handled it in the name of Jesus Christ.

One time Hensley knelt down and prayed, asking the Lord that if the signs were for today, let a rattlesnake come out of the snow. It was winter then, with snow on the ground. A rock wall was near where he was praying. As Hensley was praying, the Lord spoke to a rattlesnake that was hibernating in the rock wall. The serpent woke up and crawled out of its den, into the snow and crawled up to where Hensley was kneeling. He reached and got it and handled it in the name of Jesus Christ.

His last service in which was being held in an old blacksmith's shop, someone brought a large diamondback rattler.

The service began with singing and as Hensley listened to the singing he knew this was to be his last service. During his sermon, he went to the serpent box and got the serpent out and started handling it in the name of Jesus Christ. The rattler bit him on the hand and its venom moved through Hensley's body so fast that soon he was on the floor, writhing in agony. His faith was strong in Jesus Christ—every pain in his body that he suffered, all the persecution, all the times he spent in jail, and the times before the judges—eternal life would be worth it all. Hensley died forty-five minutes later. His funeral was held three days later in Georgia. There were 300 people there who vowed to continue handling serpents in their services.

Hensley was a great man of God. He obeyed the gospel of Jesus Christ. He laid his life down for the gospel. Revelation 14:13 says, "And I heard a voice from heaven saying unto me, Write, Blessed are the dead which die in the Lord from henceforth: Yea, said the Spirit, that they may rest from their labours, and their works do follow them." Hensley is dead and buried in his grave—resting from his labor, awaiting the second coming of Jesus Christ and a resurrection from the dead. Hensley is dead but his works do follow him. The serpent handling is very much alive today as it was nearly 2000 years go, when Jesus Christ said to go in all the world and to preach the gospel and these signs would follow the believers.

At a service at the Church of the Lord Jesus, in 1963, Sister Chaffin was bitten by a rattler and died four days later. This was the first death in the signs in West Virginia. In 1973, at the Holiness Church of God in Jesus' Name, Jimmy Williams and Buford Pack died of drinking the deadly thing. These are the only deaths that have happened by drinking poison—I have seen poison being drunk by the gallon with no harm to the one drinking it.

One man, somewhere in Kentucky, was bitten by a copperhead and died ten minutes later.

Richard Williams got bitten in a service in 1974 and died the next day—this was in Virginia.

Oscar Pelfery got bitten in a service at Big Stone Gap, Virginia, in 1968, and died eight hours later.

In the seventies, Claude Amos got bitten by a rattler that was almost 5 foot long, in Hyden, Kentucky, and died the next day.

Erin Long got bitten in a service in Harlan, Kentucky, and died. Burlin Barbee got bitten in a service in Georgia and died twelve hours later.

In the eighties, Johnny Holbrook got bitten in a service and died. Leon Johnson got bitten in a service and died twenty minutes later.

In the eighties, Richard Barrett got bitten in Georgia and died five hours later.

In 1985, Charles Prince got bitten in a service in Greeneville, Tennessee, and died two days later.

Mark Daniel got bitten in a service in Kentucky and died a few seconds later.

Melinda Brown got bit by a rattlesnake at the 1995 Middlesboro, Kentucky, homecoming and died a few days later.

Punkin Brown, Melinda's husband, died from a serpent bite he received at a revival on Sand Mountain in 1998. Melinda and Punkin are the only husband and wife couple to have both died from serpent bites.

In over a hundred years of serpent handling I know only about thirty deaths in the signs. All these men and women died for what they believed in and they hoped for resurrection at the second coming of Jesus Christ. In Matthew 10:39 it says, "He that findeth his life shall lose it: and he that loseth his life for my sake shall find it."

The newspapers love to report on deaths from serpent bites. They also like to report instances of bites and of conflict between those who handle serpents and scoffers who do not believe in the practice. I will cite a few examples.

One story appeared in the *Newport Plain Talk*. It told how
Hobart Wilford died of a snake bite. It said that the funeral
services of Hobart Wilford of Newport were held Wednesday
afternoon at 2:30 at Indian Creek Holiness church of God near
Indian Creek Docks on Douglas Lake. It said he was a tenant on
the farm of his father-in-law, Charley Pruett. Mr. Wilord was
forty-six. He was bitten by a rattlesnake Monday morning; when
he was handling the reptile at the funeral service of his brother-
in-law, Walter H. Henry, aged fifty-four. Walter died Saturday
night, a week after he had been bitten by a rattler during a
demonstration of faith in a service being at Cleveland,
Tennessee. Mr. Henry married Leote Wilford. They had lived in
Cleveland for some time. Mr. Wilford went to Cleveland alone
by bus Friday morning, after hearing that his brother-in-law had
been bitten, Saturday, August 24. When Mr. Henry died. Mr.
Wilford stayed over for the funeral services. Mr. Wilford had
been a member of the holiness faith for about four years and had
handled rattlers at the church services several times. His is the
third death caused within about three weeks from rattlesnake
bites at the Cleveland services. Harry Skelton an eighteen-year-
old minister of the church was bitten August and died August 25.
According to the Associated Press dispatches from Cleveland,
Mr. Wilford died ninety minutes after he was bitten. Services for
Mr. Wilford were conducted by his pastor, Reverend W. H.
Farner. Burial took place in the nearby cemetery. It was
understood that no faith demonstrations were to held at the
church Wednesday afternoon.

Mr. Wilford was the son of the late Mr. James Wilford. He
is survived by his wife, Leote Wilford, and six children: Lepolian,
Sarah Mae, Ruby Maggie, Leon Frances, and James. He is also
survived by three brothers—Walter, Tom and Frank, all of
Cleveland—and a sister, Anna Mae.

At the service in Kentucky when the time came for the
snakes to be handle the members would come up to the platform.
The preacher would open the box, reach in, and get the
rattlesnake out to pass it to the hands of the members that were

in the Spirit of Jesus. Music and shouting would accompany this
service. The one desiring to demonstrate that his was the
strongest would take the most deadly reptile by shifting it from
hand to hand. He would coil it around his neck and hold its darting
head near his face or body. Among the active members on this
occasion were F. D. Amburgey and his nearly eighteen-year-old
son, Dash Day Amburgey. Dash was bitten on his thumb by a
rattlesnake. He was overcome by nausea and had to be assisted
home by relatives. Upon hearing that the boy had been bitten by
the rattler, his uncle Cuba Amburgey was angered and attempted
to reach the snake and kill it. However, he was led away by his
brothers and a deputy sheriff. Amburgey was told to leave the
meeting but returned in less than one hour with his gun. Upon
his return, he was discovered stunning at the tent entrance
watching the final part of the services which followed the snake
handling. While in this position the sound of three pistol shots in
quick succession were heard out of the darkness behind the stage
end of the tent. One bullet struck Arco Angel in the back and
went entirely through his body, coming of his abdomen near his
navel. The wound was fatal. The shooting threw the crowd into a
panic and the service ended. A thirteen-year-old boy, Junior
McIntosh, said that he was standing in the tent entrance
watching Cuba Amburgey to see what he was going to do. Cuba
and another man were standing out from the corner of the tent.
They were drinking moonshine whiskey from a bottle. After
taking a drink Cuba took out his pistol and fired three shots in to
the tent at Arco Angel. The two men then ran immediately into
the crowd passing the boy within 3 feet.

Another newspaper told of this same snake handling murder
case that occurred in 1939. It said that a snake-handling religious
service that resulted in a man being killed by gunfire was a
Kentucky landmark case. It said the shooting took place near
Booneville, Kentucky. The rattlesnake handling service took
place in Lerose, Kentucky. During this period, religious services
were taking place among the Church of God in Jesus' Name and
the Churches of God. The Church of God was quite prevalent

across the Kentucky mountains during the early 1900s. Kentucky
state law bans snake handling during religious services. Handlers
believe the law violates the US Constitution and their freedom of
religion.

Cuba Amburgey of Kentucky killed Arco Angel during a
snake handling service. During this time, there was a church on
the hill in Ravena where members handled serpents. Today in
the year 2003 in Kentucky, serpent handing is still going on.

Arco Angel was reported as being shot and killed in the act of
handling poisonous reptiles during a tent meeting at the Church
of God. It was said that he was handling poisonous reptiles as a
part of a religious ceremony introduced to Kentucky over eighty
years ago by George Hensley. The church of God attracted wide
attention as a result of this practice. Services were often held in a
tent pitched in a creek bottom near the Lerose post office. As
many as 600 members have attend ended the services. The tent
where the rites were held was rectangular in shape, with sides
about 7 feet high and with a sloping roof supported by two center
posts. At the back, an elevated platform stage had been erected
on which the members and performers, including the preacher,
were stationed. This platform extended entirely across the end of
the tent and faced two tiers of crude benches separated by a
center aisle. On the night of the service the capacity of the tent
was far too small for the crowd. In order to accommodate the
large crowd so they could see the ceremony on the platform, the
right side wall and front-end wall looking from the stage were
rolled up from the ground and fastened.

Another newspaper reported on serpent handling at Jolo,
West Virginia. It said that brothers were arrested for interrupting
a religious ceremony. It said that two brothers upset with a third
brother's membership in a snake-handling sect were arrested
after barging into a church service. Seven poisonous snakes were
seized, authorities said. McDowell County sheriff's deputy R. I.
Blevins and that Steven Hagerman, aged twenty-four, and Allen
Hagerman, aged twenty-nine, of Jolo interrupted a Saturday night
service at the Church of the Lord Jesus, seizing seven poisonous

snakes, which they later killed. They were charged in magistrate court with disturbing a religious worship. Blevins said they were arrested on the same charges in the early 1980s. Blevins said the misdemeanor is punishable by up to six months in jail and $100 fine. Jeffrey Hagerman, twenty-two, is a member of the Church of the Lord Jesus, Blevins said. There was no answer at Steven Hagerman's home Tuesday. The younger brother had been bitten by poisonous snakes three or four times during similar rituals over the past four months at the church. State law in West Virginia does not forbid snake-handling services, said Magistrate Ron McKenzie, who signed the warrants against the Hagerman's on both occasions. The sect's rituals are inspired by a passage from the Bible in the Gospel of Mark. The church is a fixture in the community and has about thirty-five members, said Barbara Elkins, the wife of Pastor Joe Robert Elkins. The pastor was unavailable for comment Tuesday. Serpents are the visible sign of the devil. Mrs. Elkins said that Jesus says to take up serpents. "He didn't promise us we wouldn't be hurt," she said. In 1962 one of the Elkin's daughters, Columbia, died at age twenty-two after suffering snakebites during a service. Pastor Elkins has been bitten about twenty times, Mrs. Elkins about seventeen times and a son, Dewey Chafin, has been bitten one hundred and sixty seven times, she said. They continue to worship with the snakes. Mrs. Elkins said, "You don't think I would take those words out of scripture if I could. People die every which way. Anything we do in our worship is in the Bible. Other parishioners have from bites suffered during the ceremonies, Blevins said. No charges have been filed against the church. Blevins said the Jolo believers have taken a scripture from the Bible about people with faith in the Lord being able to handle the deadly serpents. They use snakes in their rituals. Rattlesnakes were seized in the two raids. The two Hagerman brothers stringently objected to the other brother's involvement in the church. Steven and Allen Hagerman were released on their own recognizance, said Magistrate Shirley Pickett. No hearing was set because both have requested court-appointed attorneys, she said.

Even though newspaper continue to report on bites and troubles within the Jesus' Name churches, we will not change how we believe. Man has made a law against the true gospel of Jesus Christ with the signs following the believers because of a few deaths that happened in the signs. But man does not make a law against the killing of little babies inside the mother's womb. It is said that 4000 babies are killed each day in the United States; there have been over 12 million babies killed. The doctors and all that have partakers in killing babies and the women that have done this will stand before Jesus Christ, at the last judgment, for the babies that have been murdered. In Revelation 20:11–15 it says,

> And I saw a great white throne, and him that sat on it, from whose face the earth and heaven fled away; and there was found no place for them. And I saw the dead, small and great, stand before God and the books were opened, and another book was opened, which is the book of life, and the dead were judged out of those things, which were written in the books, according to their works. And the sea gave up the dead, which were in it, and death and hell delivered up the dead which were in them, and they were cast into the lake of fire, This is the second death. And whosever was not found written in the book of life was cast into the lake of fire. And if they don't Repent, of their sins the lake of fire will be their home.

On Friday, October 18, 1985, at the House of Prayer in Jesus' Name in Morristown, Tennessee, I preached from the book of Matthew, chapters 5, 6, and 7. Jesus Christ gave victory over a rattlesnake. Brother Marvin Gregg, John Fish, John Brown, Jr. (from Georgia), and I got anointed to take up the serpent.

On October 19, 1985, in Marshall, North Carolina, at the House of Prayer in the Name of Jesus Christ, John Brown, who is pastor there, had the Lord's Supper and foot washing. We had one cup that we all drank from. We had a great time in the Lord.

On October 20, 1985, at the House of Prayer in Jesus' Name in Kentucky, the service got started at seven in the evening. The serpents at that service were an 8-foot cobra, a two-step viper, three large rattlers (two black and one yellow), five copperheads, and one pygmy rattler and a cottonmouth. Jesus Christ gave victory to me and to Jim Carr, Marvin Gregg, John Brown, John Brown, Jr., and five more brothers that I did not know. We had victory over the 8-foot cobra and the rest of the serpents. After we prayed, the service came to an end.

Today there are churches in fifteen states that handle serpents and are still growing in numbers. The Bible said that the gospel of His kingdom with the signs following shall be preached unto all the world. Then shall the end come. Our religion has already gone into many nations across the sea. I don't know how long it will take, but the gospel that Jesus Christ preached, the gospel of the kingdom of God with the signs following the believers, is going to be preached all over the world. I don't care how much the law and other people fight the true gospel—it is going to be preached.

# Chapter 9

"I will praise thee O Lord, among the people: and I will sing praise unto thee among the nations." (Psalm 108:3)

# Brother Colonel Hartman Bunn and the Zion Tabernacle

This is the story of Colonel Hartman Bunn as he told it to me. Hartman Bunn was born near Zebulon in North Carolina. He was the son of a farmer. He was named Colonel by his parents. He took the middle name Hartman for himself when he was in school. It symbolizes his calling to preach which he first felt when he was about seven years old. He was brought up in the faith of a Missionary Baptist church. At the age of seventeen, he become aware that the church was not in the sanctification doctrine and withdrew his membership. About twenty years of preaching in tent revival meeting in some twenty-two states along the east coast followed. This early preaching was done with the Church of God group, which began in Cleveland, Tennessee. Bunn came to Durham in 1930. He did all kinds of construction work, preaching on the side. He still does some construction and brick-laying work, although pastoring the Zion Tabernacle takes most of his time. The members are allied to the Holiness Church of God in Jesus Christ Name in spirit but are independent. Other churches in North Carolina in the thirties were chartered as the Church of God, Jesus' Name People, Inc. The name was chosen more for the purpose of obtaining the charter and is hardly known by many of those who attend the church meetings. In other churches, pride and greed robbed the spirit of God of its sweetness and purity. Long ago the church had no membership basis. In Acts 2:38 it says, "Peter said unto them repent, and be baptized every one of you in the name of Jesus Christ for the remission of sins and ye shall receive the gift of the Holy Ghost." In Acts 2:47 it says, "Then the Lord added to the church daily such as should be saved."

There are churches in Durham, Winston-Salem, and Henderson. There also are meeting in other states and cities. The membership of these churches numbers in the thousands. Today there are churches in twenty-five states. Financial matters are handled by a treasurer. The treasurer for the Durham church was Cornelius Higgs. There are no collections or planned money drives. Most of the money comes from the regular members. Bunn said that the curious who flock to the meeting add very little to the collection plate. The affairs of the church are in the hands of the faithful according to their various abilities. There are no elected deacons or elders.

Serpent-handling churches are independent and free. Some publish their articles of faith, often posting them on the church wall. For example, the Holiness Church of God in Jesus' Name in Big Stone Gap, Virginia.

# The Holiness Church of God in Jesus' Name
## (Big Stone Gap, Virginia)
# Articles of Faith

Article I

Section 1. The Lord He is God. Psalms 100:3, Isaiah 43:10, Luke 2:11, Acts 2:36

Article II

Water Baptism In the Name of the Lord Jesus Christ. Mathew 28:19, Acts 2:38, Col. 3:1.

Article III

Baptism of the Holy Ghost. Joel 2:28, 29; Acts 2:2, 3, 4.

Article IV

The Lord's Supper. Genesis 14:18, Matthew 26:26, 27, 28, 29; 1st Cor. 11:23, 24, 25, 26.

Article V

Birth of the Spirit. Isaiah 66:8, 9; St. John 3:3, 45; 1st Cor. 12:13.

Article VI

The Washing of Feet. St. John 13, 1 Timothy 5:10, 1 Peter 2:21.

Article VII

These Signs shall follow them that Believe. Casting out devils. Mark 16:17, Luke 10:17, Acts 5:16.

New Tongues. Mark 16:17, Acts 2:4, Acts 10:46.

They shall take up Serpents. Genesis 3:14, Acts 28:5, Mark 16:18.

If they drink any deadly thing it shall not hurt them. Mark 16:18, Luke 10:19, Mark 9:23.

Laying hands on the sick. Mark 16:18, Acts 9:17, James 5:14.

Article VIII

If a woman have long hair it is a glory to her, for her hair is given her for a covering. 1 Cor. 11:5 through 16, St. John 12:1, Timothy 2:9, 1 Peter 3:3.

Article IX

Second Coming of Christ. Daniel 7:13, Acts 1:11, Rev. 1:7.

Article X

Tithes and offerings. Genesis 14:20, Malachi 3:10, Heb. 7.

Article XI

The Resurrection of the just and unjust. Daniel 12:2, St. John 5:28, 29; Rev. 20:12.

Article XII

The Way of Holiness. Isaiah 35:8, Luke 1:74, 75; Heb. 12:14

Article XIII

Section 1. To greet or salute. To greet with a holy kiss. 1 Samuel 10:1, Romans 16:16; 2 Cor. 13:12; 1 Thess. 5:26; 1 Peter 5:14.

Section 2. To greet by name. 1 Samuel 25:5; 3 John 1:14. Greeting by letter. Col. 4:18; 2 Thess. 3:17, James 1:1.

Section 3. Order of greeting with a holy kiss is for the brother to greet brother and sister to greet sister, brother to greet sister by hand shake. Sister to greet brother by name or hand shake. 1 Cor. 14:40; 1 Cor. 6:12; 1 Cor. 10:23; 1 Cor. 13:5.

Article XIV

The speaking of the spirit. 2 Samuel 23:2, 3; Luke 1:70; Acts 8:29, Acts 10:19, 20; Acts 13:2.

Article XV

The use of Tobacco. Ministers should not use tobacco. Phil 3:17; 1 Timothy 4:12. Members should not use tobacco. 1 Cor. 11:1; 2 Thess. 3:9, Romans 14:20, 21.

At one service, Bunn preached that the Bible refers to the eleventh chapter of Hebrews in the Old Testament times where Shadrack, Messhack, and Abednego were cast into a fiery furnace and didn't even have their eyebrows singed. Bunn passed serpents out to the members that were anointed to handle them. Mrs. Hettie Davidson, a black woman of Winston-Salem, handled aloft a giant timberback rattlesnake by the anointing of God. She was the only black woman in the congregation. That made the headlines in the Durham Sunday paper. Oscar Hutton, a member of a Jesus' Name Church from St. Charles, Virginia, held the Bible in one hand and serpents in the other.

At the opening of a three-day service in Durham North Carolina people entered the church one Sunday night. Inside the church were rows of hard wooden benches. Pastor Colonel Hartman Bunn was dressed in a black suit and wearing a tie which was held in place with a gold tie-clasp He walk to the front of the church and greeted the crowd. Ministers from the church of God in Jesus' Name took the lead in the Sunday services. Edward Noah of High Point, North Carolina, and L. D. Tripp of Jonesboro, North Carolina, were there. Oscar Hutton, Jack Parson and Paul Dotson, all of St Charles, Virginia, was also there. Police came to the church and what happened was reported in the Durham, North Carolina, paper.

The article was headed by "Snake Seized at Tabernacle to be Tested." It said that Chief of Police H. E. King left for Raleigh about mid-morning today, carrying with him five poisonous-type snakes seized by police last night during a serpent-handling service at Colonel Hartman Bunn's Zion Tabernacle Church on Peabody Street. It went on to say that Chief King said that the snakes would be tested by experts in Raleigh to determine if their "venom ejecting equipment" was intact. If the examinations reveal that the serpents actually are poisonous warrants will be issued for five members of the church alleged by police to have handled the reptiles during the church services last night. Bunn and Oscar Hutton were named among the five who were known to have handled the serpents. The paper stated that as the officers stalked into the packed building; Hutton had several snakes wrapped around his neck and was reaching for more. A young woman had a small copperhead in her hand. Bunn and others had been handling the copperhead a few moments before.

Colonel Bunn said he handled his first serpent in 1946. He was working out by his barn when he spotted a poisonous moccasin. The anointing of Jesus Christ came over him. It said he felt a spiritual feeling and joy in his soul. He called it "glorified happiness." Mr. Bunn told me that "all of a sudden with that spiritual feeling on me; I reached down with my hand and picked up that highland moccasin; he didn't even flick his tongue."

Bunn become the pastor of the Zion Tabernacle Church. He held services on Peabody Street Saturday and Sunday evenings beginning at 7:30. Mrs. C. H. Bunn announced that rattlesnakes and copperheads will be used in the services. Bunn preached and declared that he had the gift of discerning of spirit. He said that four weeks ago he was in the spirit and felt that he was about to win a major victory. At that time he said he knew nothing about snakes. A Henderson man brought some snakes from West Virginia, rattlesnakes and copperheads. He was especially anointed by God for the handling of the serpents. Bunn said the only gift he had was the Anointing of the Spirit of God. He said that the handling of the serpents according to the gospel of Mark and the Acts of the Apostles are the only signs for believers. Bunn preached other signs are healing, casting out the devil, and speaking in new tongues. He also has feet washing. All services follow the Spirit. Bunn said he doesn't plan to test his faith by drinking strychnine. He said, "I don't profess to know everything but it doesn't sound-like to me that the scripture ever commanded or suggested the drinking of poison." Bunn preached that the Bible says, "and if they drink any deadly thing it shall not hurt them." It does not command anyone to actually drink poison. He said people should only handle serpents when anointed. He preached that he would be afraid to handle poisonous snakes unless he had the anointing of God. He said nobody else should pick up a serpent unless he or she was anointed. Bunn preached he had never been called upon to handle fire as a test of faith because he said, "I've never claimed victory over fire."

Colonel Bunn has been in the papers many times due to laws against the handling of serpents in Durham, North Carolina. One time the paper read, "Law prohibits They Shall Take up Serpents." It said that Colonel Hartman Bunn, pastor of the Zion Tabernacle in Durham, North Carolina, came into prominence in the fall of 1947 when the law in city's ordinance against Mark 16, "they shall take up serpents." Police staged their first raid at the faith Zion Tabernacle the night of November 1, 1947. The paper went on to say how Captain Glenn Rosemond used a metal-pronged rod to seize two frisky copperheads and drop them into a metal can. The serpents were taken by the health department officials to the curator or the state museum in Raleigh. After examining them the curator said they were normal copperheads. He said they were dangerous with fangs intact. Several days later in the basement of the courthouse a pair of white rats were placed on a floor in front of the snakes. The copperheads quickly struck the frightened rodents, both of whom died within twenty minutes. At all of his meetings, Bunn voiced nothing but respect for the police and requested his followers not to speak ill of city council. "We love everybody," he emphasized. Bunn was fined $50 for violation of the snake ordinance. Bunn refused to pay the fine and elected to take a thirty-day jail sentence. He declined the offer of money by his congregation to pay the fine.

Behind bars Bunn studied his Bible, drew plans for a house he later built with his own hands, and conceded he was having a needed rest. Bunn later appealed his conviction to the State Supreme Court, which eventually upheld the conviction. While free under bond, Bunn held services off the courthouse steps surrounded by his followers. Smartly dressed in a navy blue double-breasted suit, Bunn's ringing voice and guitar strumming, was backed up by a church member who played the accordion. They attracted hundreds to the scene and for a while blocked traffic. After the court ventures, Bunn's activities subsided, or so the police said. However the truth is that Bunn and his followers moved to a clearing in a wooded sector in the county off Raleigh Road where copperheads and rattlesnakes were plentiful. He returned to action along with chants and strange mumblings and writhing by the congregation. In the spring of 1948, Bunn began assisting in services in a Winston-Salem church where he said that serpents were in evidence. The congregation was made up of about one-fourth black people.

In October 1948, a three-day faith healing service was staged in the Zion Tabernacle with venomous serpents. Followers of the Church of God in Jesus' Name came from Virginia, Tennessee, and Kentucky. A squadron of police burst into the church and seized four fat copperheads and a rattler. Bunn asked them to arrest him, but this time they ignored him. Moans and wails of anguish followed captain Rosemond and his men as they left with the serpents, which had to be examined and found poisonous before a warrant could be issued for an arrest. These manmade laws are a violation of our religious freedom.

The first amendment contains two distinct clauses designed to protect religious freedom. One is the establishment clause, which prohibits any law respecting the establishment of religion. The other is the free exercise clause, which bans laws prohibiting the free exercise of religion.

*Everson vs. Board of Education* said no one may be punished for entertaining or professing religious beliefs or disbeliefs, church attendance or non-attendance. The government may not prefer one religion to another.

When Bunn and another church member, Benjamin Ralph Massey of Henderson, were found guilty of violating the Durham's new ordinance banning the handling in church of poisonous snakes neither was represented by counsel. Both entered pleas of not guilty when their cases were called. When Bunn was assessed a fine of $50 and costs, he appealed in the name of religious freedom. During the appeal, his bond was set at $100. In a statement to the court at the conclusion of the state's evidence, Bunn reasserted his belief in Mark 16:18 ("they shall take up serpents"). He stated that the city ordinance was unconstitutional and reiterated his intention to appeal to the state supreme court.

Bunn then asked how they knew Bunn he had handled the snake "willfully" as stated in the warrant. "You had had him in your hands" was the reply. "How do you know that the spirit was not on me and caused me to handle the snake?" Bunn replied. The judge interrupted at that point. He said that the point was not material to the case

Bunn insisted that he had to plead not guilty because "I am not guilty." He said he did not handle the snake of his own volition. "The sweetest reason why I pleaded not guilty is because God took the fear of snakes away from me and caused me to handle them," he asserted after the trial was over.

Colonel Hartman Bunn has handled serpents for over twenty years without being hurt. It's the power of God that allows him to take up serpents. I have handle serpents in the name of Jesus Christ for over thirty years. A Duke University anthropologist, Dr. Weston LaBarre (who has written a book on serpent handlers), believes there's a natural explanation for the handling of serpents. If he believes his natural explanation, why doesn't he pick up the serpents?

Conflicting views about the handling of the serpents were offered by scholars at a full-scale academic analysis of the religions of the Bible Belt held at Duke University in the late 1940s. LaBarre discussed "some oddities" of Southern religion. He said one of the oddest is the use of serpents as a part of Christian worship. He claimed it still is practiced, sometimes openly and sometime secretly, in remote churches scattered across Appalachia. Dr. LaBarre said with laws in many areas prohibiting serpent handling it has declined massively after hitting a peak in the 1950s. But Dr. LaBarre and the scholars are wrong. I know today (in the year 2003) of at least fifty churches

that still handle serpents. Colonel Hartman Bunn, pastor of Zion
Tabernacle, said he knew of congregations in a half dozen
Southern states where venomous serpents are regularly handled in
the midst of religious services. "I still do it myself on occasion,"
he said, "despite a local ordinance against it. It's spiritual
experience. It's also in the scriptures by no less an authority than
Jesus Christ. I believe it." He noted that in Mark 16:18 Jesus says
a sign of those who believe will be that they shall take up
serpents without being harmed. He also noted that in Luke 10:19,
he promises the power to tread on serpents and scorpions
unscathed and also over other enemy forces. Bunn stated that
"Only a few times have I felt anointed to take off my shoes and
walk on them." Reverend Bunn commented that without the
Spirit protecting you, you are lost.

At his conference, Dr. LaBarre never said anything about all
the people that are killed in wars, famines, and pestilences. He
didn't say anything about the AIDS disease that will kill millions
or the wide extent of sexual promiscuity.

Dr. LaBarre did say deaths by serpent bites in church have
been extremely few. This raises the question as to why don't the
poisonous rattlers, copperheads, and cottonmouth moccasins bite
their handlers? Dr. LaBarre maintained that snakes strike toward
the point of a warm body, but when handle and coil around such a
body they can't focus. It upsets their neurology. Snakes bite
when they sense heat. Snakes have a Jacob gland in their head to
detect heat. They will bite only when they feel heat. Dr. LaBarre
also said snakes are accustomed to coiling but they can't coil while
being handled. The reasons snakes don't bite are thus completely
naturalistic according to Dr. LaBarre. Dr. LaBarre claimed that
serpent handlers provide an example of a primitive religion in a
twentieth-century setting. LaBarre characterized the followers of
our tradition as backward, impressionable, intellectually-deprived
people. He said it was implausible that anybody would believe
such garbage.

Of course, Dr. LaBarre never picked up the snake to show
how his natural explanation works to keep a snake from biting. In

my forty-six year I have seen snakes open their mouth just lying and strike. Snake don't have to coil to bite. If they are in the hand of a handler the snake just open its mouth and bite.

Reverend Bunn also disputed the naturalistic explanation of Dr. LaBarre. Bunn noted that the academic does not accept the fact that faith is needed to successfully handle serpents. He explained that faith gives us power over everything. "I am just as afraid of snake as the next man," he said. "If one crawled in this room and the spiritual anointment wasn't with me, I'd climb up on the roof."

Academics like LaBarre and believers like Colonel Hartman Bunn will forever be at odds. If one will not accept the Word of God, they must seek elsewhere for explanations. But we who believe and know God's word have the only answer we need. That is why as long as there is God's word there will be believers who take up serpents.

# Chapter 10

"But and if you suffer for righteousness' sake happy are ye and be not afraid of their terror, neither be troubled." (1 Peter 3:14)

## The Bite of a Young Man at the Sand Hill Church of God in Jesus' Name

The Sand Hill Church of God in Jesus' Name was built in 1949. The Raines family lived on Sol-Messer Mountain. It is a ragged, torn, and tattered road into the mountain. The Raines family lived about half way up the mountain in a old cabin that set on the right side the road. My great grandma, Nancy Leatherwood, owned a cabin to the left. You had to walk in because the road that lead into her place (called the Buddy Turner place) was so ragged. The mountain has not changed much in the last fifty years except that the cabins are all about rotted down so that you would never know that anybody ever lived there. The only things that remain of the cabins are the corner rocks that used to hold up the cabin. There are a few old broken dishes lying in the tall weeds.

On Saturday, August 4, 1951, life was everywhere. People lived back in every hollow. August mornings in the hills of East Tennessee are real warm and the nights are hot and muggy. That morning started as any other day—getting up, getting dressed, eating breakfast, and doing the morning chores. Back in Buddy Hollow at grandma's place, they were working the tobacco field, topping the plants so they would spread out and have bigger leafs. While working in the tobacco field, my grandma Bertha

Arrington killed a big old copperhead. She told me some thirty years later that she felt that someone was going to get bit that night (Saturday, August 4, 1951).

She was looking forward to the Saturday service at Sand Hill Church of God in Jesus' Name. It was some 6 miles down the road. At about 4 miles there is a short cut through the old Ikeie Coggins' place. You can go through those woods and come out to Big Creek. You have to walk the log to cross the creek to get to the church. As a boy I have walked through the woods and across that log many of a time hunting with my cousin for coons. You came out behind the church.

As the day was coming to a close and the evening was drawing on people started to the church. They came from the hollows and mountains where they lived. That night Lester Raines took two copperheads that Blackburn had caught early that week for the church service. Lester had a hole dug out in the bank at the back of his cabin. My uncle Hastel Presnell said that he saw six rattlesnakes and four copperhead in a cage back in the bank where Lester lived.

The church was small, about 22 by 31 feet. They lighted the church with gas lamps. That night the church house was full of people from everywhere. Oscar Pelfery, Jacky Euel Blackburn, Oll McMahan, and family all from Virginia. Also there were Alvin Hall, Carl Hall and family, Cora James, Edward Lee Turner and family. Other people at church that night were Joe Frank Turner and family Lester Raines and family, Mary Turner and family, Ed Arrwood, Riley Arrwood and family, and Sarah Turner, Della Mae Turner. Leote Wilford was also there with her children, Lepolian, Sarah Mae, Ruby, Maggie, Leon, Fances, and James. Several more families were there.

Service got started with the congregation singing. Then they had prayer request and there was prayer. They also had special singing. About that time Mullins from Virginia carried up front a big black rattlesnake in a box and set it next to a box with two copperheads in it. Jacky Euel Blackburn, Lester Raines, Oscar Pelfery, Oll McMahan, and Mullins were sitting up front.

Someone moved the serpent boxes and set them on the piano bench. Johnny Raines was singing "Jacob's Ladder" when Blackburn went to the serpent box and got the two copperheads out. After he handled them, he put the copperheads back in the box. He opened the box that had the big large timberback rattlesnake in it. Gladys told me it was as big as a man's arm and over 6 feet long. As Blackburn was a handling it, he put it around Johnny's shoulder. The snake crawled down Johnny's arm. The large rattlesnake struck Johnny on the right hand. Johnny let the serpent fall to the floor. Lester picked it up and put it back in the box. A few seconds after the serpent bit Johnny, he started to sink to the floor. He got real sick and passed out. The church member started praying for him. Still Johnny he got worse. They got him down to Valintine Shults where they talked Lester Raines into taking his son to the hospital. Johnny was only fifteen years old when he got bit.

On Monday, August 6, 1951, the *Newport Plain Talk* had an article headed "Warrant Issued for Snake Handler: Lad Bitten: Reported Seriously." It said that the boy has fair chance of recovery. It went on to say that a warrant was issued this Monday morning by Esquire Walter Layman against Jacky Blackburn, a so-called preacher from Virginia, charging him with handling and displaying poisonous snakes to the endangerment of lives and health of others. Officers were requested to destroy the rattlesnake if it was sill in the county. The officers went to the Sand Hill Church of God in Jesus' Name and found the two copperheads and the big rattlesnake behind the church in the weeds. They got them and put them in the car and up the old 15th where they stopped at Timman Ball's store. Timman told me some thirty-five years ago there was venom all over the inside of the box. The rattlesnake that was in it would bite the box it was so mean.

The newspaper said that the preacher held services at the Sand Hill Church of God in Jesus' Name on August 4, 1951, Saturday night in the eighth district. It reported that the preacher threw a snake on young Raines'son. It said the lad was bitten on the right hand and is now in a local hospital in a serious condition. The officers reported that Blackburn is being held in the Cocke County Jail on a misdemeanor charge pending the condition of Johnny. Officers searched for and destroyed the three snakes reported to have been used in the service. The warrant was issued under a 1947 anti-snake handling law. This law makes it a misdemeanor to handle or display snakes in a way that the lives or health of people might be endangered. The punishment is a fine of not less that $50 nor more than $150 dollars and by imprisonment in the county jail.

I believe that this manmade 1947 law doesn't say anything about freedom of religion or the freedom of every individual to worship as he wishes. The First Amendment to US Constitution bans laws prohibiting the free exercise of religion. I believe it is our right and duty to handle serpents as it plainly states in Mark 16:18.

Later, in the same newspaper they printed a story in which Johnny Raines got to express some of our beliefs about handling scents. The article was headed "Virginian Talks Freely about Snake Handling." It said the condition of the fifteen-year-old boy, Johnny Raines who lives in the old fifteenth in the Sol Mountain community of Cocke County in Eighth District is believed to be better today than at any time since he was bitten by a big rattlesnake during a snake-handling service at Sand Hill Church of God in Jesus' Name one Saturday night. It said he remains in a local hospital where physicians have given him a fair chance of recovering. In the meantime, the newspaper said that Euel Blackburn is out on bail after being arrested and charged with handling and displaying poisonous snakes to the endangerment of lives and health of others. The reporter went on to say that Backburn who was with little Johnny at the hospital this morning told this writer that he is a preacher of the Church of God in Jesus' Name faith. He quotes scripture that the Lord will take care of Johnny. He told the reporter, "We have been praying for him and he is under the faith." Blackburn said that he was a coal miner in addition to being a preacher of the gospel. He said that he has been bitten six times and although he suffered, the Lord took care of him. Then he suggested that the following be printed from the words of Jesus in gospel of Mark: "Go ye into all the world and preaches the gospel to every creature. He that believeth and is baptized shall be saved, but he that believeth not shall be damned. And these signs shall follow them that believe. In my name shall they cast out devils, they shall speak with new tongues, they shall take up serpents, and if they drink any deadly thing it shall not hurt them; they shall lay hands on the sick and they shall recover" (Mark 15:16–18). The reporter went on to say that Euel knew it was illegal to handle serpents in church, but he said, "It is the Word of God and my faith and I have been participating in similar services for a long time." The tall lanky Virginian said, "I even had my picture in *Life Magazine* during a service. It was a pretty good picture, too." When asked about drinking deadly things he said that he drinks strychnine in special services, but has not done so in Cocke County. He also said that "I don't mind what the people say about me. I don't mind having my picture in the paper. After all, this is what I believe." He said he was arrested once before. Blackburn said that there was a large crowd at the church services Saturday night and when his boy was bitten a lot of them got excited. He added that after Johnny was bitten they started praying.

The reporter went on to say that Johnny was asleep during most of the morning and did not talk with the reporter. His face was swollen and so was his right hand where he was bitten. Johnny had after promised to let the reporter know when similar services are to be held. Blackburn asked the reporter to save a copy of the article and any pictures used of him.

The local newspapers continued to cover the story. In an article headed " Snake Handler Jackie Raines Bound Over in Friday Hearing." The story began, "Euel Jacky Blackburn charged." It said a young Cocke County boy was bitten during services at the Sand Hill Church of God in Jesus' Name was bound over to circuit court on a one thousand dollar bond. The newspaper reported that a very large crowed of interested citizens were present for the trial. It reported that the state explained to the court the inadequacy of the law enacted by the Tennessee legislature to prohibit snake handling in services. It claimed an indictment against Reverend Euel Blackburn would be sought for a felonious assault at the next session of Cocke County grand jury. It reported that the maximum fine for the offense is $150. In addition it noted that the trial judge can add up to six months in the county workhouse. Attorney Fred Myers and criminal investigator Roy Campbell, Jr., represented the state.

The newspaper coverage continued with an article headed "Snake Handler Blackburn Gets Six Months in Workhouse and One Hundred Dollar Fine." The article reported that Euel was fined $100 in circuit court and given a sentence of six months in the workhouse after he was convicted of handling snakes in violation of Tennessee state law. The story noted that Euel's trial grew out of his arrest following snake handling services at the Sand Hill Church of God in Jesus' Name when a fifteen-year-old boy was bitten and had to remain in the hospital for several weeks. It reported that a witness said that he saw Blackburn place the snake around the boy's shoulder. The witness said that he saw the snake bite the boy.

The newspaper went on to say that in sentencing the defendant the judge pointed out that the Tennessee State Supreme Court has upheld the law, which prohibits the handling of snakes. The newspaper also reported that five persons were indicted before the grand jury on a charge of handling snakes. It noted that although the case was not on the docket at this time, it is possible that these persons will be tried during this term of court. The jury set a fine of $100. It said he matter of a jail sentence was a matter for the court to decide. The maximum sentence was given. Euel was told that after serving seventy-five days in the workhouse, he would be eligible to be released. The newspaper reported that the judge warned Euel that any violation of the law during the parole time or thereafter meant that he would have to serve the remaining time of the sentence.

The newspapers continued to show interest in the recovery of Johnny. In an article headed "Johnny Is Holding His Own: Doctor Reports Today" it was noted that Johnny's physician said that he is holding his own, but added that he is still in critical condition and must remain in the hospital. The newspaper noted that Johnny was in his third week in his fight against death. The newspaper reported that due to the seriousness of his injury the young teenager was unable to appear at the preliminary trial of Blackburn. The newspaper reported that the prosecuting attorneys stated then that in the event the young lad dies, Blackburn would be placed under a charge of murder. The newspaper went on to report that thousands of Cocke County citizens are anxious about the young boy who lives in the 8th district and have called this paper. The paper noted that Johnny's physician stated that it was the most sever case of a snakebite that he has ever seen. He claimed that even if Johnny lived he would be permanently disabled.

In another article headed "Snake Handlers Busy Here During Weekend," it was noted that three affidavits were presented to the attorney general stating that over the weekend Johnny who but a few days ago lingered near death from snakebite was well enough to sing the chorus of "Jacobs Ladder" for an audience composed of his family and several nurses at the local clinic where he is a patient. The paper reported that Johnny was in high spirits but still a very sick boy. With his parents at his bedside the youth was anxious to tell of his experience and insisted that it was not lack of faith that caused him to be bit. Johnny said it was just willed by God. "When I get well, and I know I will, I'll be just as willing to try again," the paper reported Johnny saying. The newspaper noted that Johnny had lost some twenty pounds since he was snake bitten. His worse time came when he suffered a relapse after showing marked improvement during the first week following the accident. "I know God will let me go home soon," Johnny was reported to have said. The newspaper reported that this nice-looking seventh-grade student is quite willing to talk about snake-handling experiences "even with his bandaged hand minus two finger." In the meantime, there have been more snake-handling services, despite the fact that five persons have already been convicted of handling.

The newspaper reported that at the Cleveland Tennessee Church of God headquarters, Homer Tomlinson, the son of A. J. Tomlinson, the first general overseer of the Church of God, claimed the church saw the wonder of taking up of the serpents in the early 1900s. The first church in Cocke County was the Carson Springs Church of God built early in the 1900s The local newspaper continued to cover the plight of serpent handling in Cocke County. In an article headed "Submissions on Unlawful Handling of Snakes Brings on Workhouse Sentences," the newspaper reported a courthouse scene of shouting as six defendants were convicted of unlawfully handling snakes. Rile and Ed Arwood, and Ida Mae, Della Mae, Sarah, and Edward Lee Turner were all sentenced. Riley and Ed Arwood were fined $50 each and given six months in jail to be suspended after serving three days. Edward Lee Turner was given the same sentence. The three women, one an elderly lady, the other a very young woman, and the third being in ill health, were each given ten dollar fines and six months sentences, suspended until they participate in such services again. The newspaper reported that Judge Shepherd tried to get the defendants to say they would refrain from further handling of snakes. He reportedly told them he was trying to find an excuse to keep from sending them to jail. However, when all indicated that they would not refrain from doing so, he told them there was nothing else he could do but follow the law. The paper reported that it appeared that the two ministers that been leading the service had fled the state and were not in custody. The paper reported the Judge as saying s that he had reports from that community that Euel Blackburn from Virginia was not a good worker, that he lived off of food and means which his mother obtained from welfare. The newspaper reported that people from the Sand Hill community went out into the hallway and shouted as the men were taken to jail.

In another newspaper article, "Sand Hill Church of God in Jesus' Name Members Invite Public to Church," the newspaper printed a letter and an invitation from Mrs. Ethel James. It said,

Dear reader if thou can believe, all things are possible. Greeting in the name of our lovely Lord and Savior Jesus Christ. We the Church of God members thank and praise God for the little church at the foot of Sand Hill in the old 15th district. We just go out to the house of God and sing and shout the wonderful praises of God. We just thank God for salvation we can feel. We cordially invite everybody to come out and hear the Word of God. We just thank God we've been sanctified by the Word of God and baptized with the Holy Ghost and are on our way to heaven, Praise God! If you have the love of God in your heart you can sing and pray for your enemy that despitefully use you. We get lots of hard things said about us, but we're serving a God that is able to carry us over, praise his holy name. 1 Peter 3:14 says, "But and if you suffer for righteous sake happy are ye and be not afraid of their terror, neither be troubled." Revelation 3:5 says, "he that over cometh the same shall be clothed in white raiment and I will not blot out his name out of the book of life, but I will confess his name before my father and before his angels." We have been called trash, but praise God, trash floats on top. We don't mind that we have been mocked. Praise God! We don't care. God says revengence is mine and I will repay. We just thank and praise his holy sweet name. We're working for a crown of glory. The world looks down upon us and says we were so rash they laugh and talk about us and say we are but trash. But we will sing and we will shout and preach the way of holiness. We will sing and shout till our precious loving savior's face we view. Mark 8:34 says, "and whosoever will come after me let him deny himself and take up his cross and follow me." Thank you.

While the local newspaper followed the fate of little Johnny and the serpent handlers of the Sand Hill Church of God in Jesus' Name, once Johnny recovered the paper lost interest in serpent handlers. Euel Blackburn went back to Virginia and fell asleep in a old cabin. It caught on fire and Blackburn was burnt up. They found the remains of his body in the burned down cabin. Some said that he died from sugar coma. Lester told me that the night the cabin burned down and Blackburn died the old oil lamps went out at the Sand Hill church.

# Chapter 11

'For I am now ready to be offered, and the time of my departure is at hand." (2 Timothy 3)

## The Holiness Church of God in Jesus' Name

The Holiness Church of God in Jesus' Name was built in 1969 in Carson Springs, Tennessee. It became notorious when newspapers covered deaths that occurred in this church. Newspapers chronicled the fate of two preaches of the gospel who died for the faith.

In an article headed "Bitten Serpent Handler Couldn't Be Better," the local newspaper reported that a Cocke County man who was bitten two weeks straight. Wednesday night snake-handling ceremonies at the Holiness Church of God in Jesus' Name in Carson Springs couldn't be healthier according to a relative, Liston Pack. The man was bitten on the hand by a copperhead two weeks ago during religious services and then again on the hand during the next service on Wednesday. He is feeling just fine, his Brother Liston Pack was reported saying Thursday. "He got up this morning and went on to work," said Liston. Buford Pack has been participating in the snake-handling ceremonies since he was saved early last year (1970). He was first bitten Wednesday night about one hour after the service had begun in the one-room church, the newspaper reported. Members also participated in the snake handling, passing a small copperhead around in a circle and shouting. The paper reported that after he returned to his seat, Buford Pack's hand and forearm began to swell. However, by Thursday morning the swelling had receded. The paper reported that Liston's brother Buford Pack was bitten on the mouth. Buford Pack never went to the doctor for the bite, believing that Jesus would keep him from being harmed by the snake. It was reported that church members said the congregation had fourteen rattlesnakes and copperheads to use in the services. Newsmen from both Knoxville newspapers who attended the services Wednesday night described the incident this way. "He turned back to the box, flipped open the end and barely stuck his hand inside when the serpent struck. Mr. Pack had been bitten on the knuckle of the thumb. 'My, you're a live one, ' Buford is reported to have said to the serpent that bit him. His hand trembled as he reached in with the other hand and dragged out the squirming reptile. He held it aloft and said, 'Praise God.'"

Another newspaper article was headed "Contempt of Court Suit Filed Against Snake Handling Church." It was published July 13, 1973. It reported that district attorney H. F. Duct expressed fears that Cocke County would become the snake-handling capital of the world. He filed contempt of court proceeding against elders of the Holiness Church of God in Jesus' Name. The petition filed in Cocke County circuit court seeks fines or prison terms for Pastor Listion Pack, and other church officials, including Drew Click, Clyde Ricker, and Alfred Ball. It was reported that the petition clams the church members disobeyed a temporary injunction granted in April by Circuit Court Judge George Shepherd barring snake handling during church services. A hearing date for the case was set for July 28 at 10:00 A.M. before Judge Shepherd. Defendants were ordered to post $100 appearance bonds to be released from custody. The newspaper quoted as follows: "This petitioner is not trying to make a martyr of said defendants, but the police power of the state of Tennessee must preserve and save human lives. The suit reportedly said that if snake handling was not stopped at this fundamental church, Cocke County Tennessee would become the snake-handling capital of the world. The suit grew out of what church members called a national convention at the Carson Springs Church, July 1 when several hundred members and

visitors from other states handled rattlesnakes and other
poisonous reptiles as part of the services.

Another newspaper article indicated that the law against
serpent handling in Tennessee was unlikely to be repealed. In
"Repeal of Snake Handling Law Impossible This Year," State
Senator Kenneth Porter of Newport, Tennessee, is reported as
saying that he could offer no assistance this year to members of
the Holiness Church of God in Jesus' Name that there would be
a repeal of a state law banning serpent handling in church. During
the hearing, Judge George R. Shepherd reportedly advised the
defendants they could seek a senator to make application to repeal
the law. Porter said he could do nothing at this time, noting the
cut-off date for introduction of any legislation in the Tennessee
General Assembly was April 18. The paper said Porter said he had
recently been the object of a practical joke in Nashville as result
of the large amount of publicity the snake-handling incident had
received. "I came into my office one morning, and there was a
Nashville newspaper there on my desk," he is reported to have
said. "It had a large circle drawn around a story about the church
here. I picked the paper up, looked at it and threw it down. Then
I looked down and saw a five or six foot long snake somebody had
put in my office. It was rubber but it scared the hell out of me."

In the *Newport Plain Talk* of Monday, April 9, 1973, an
article appeared headed "Two Holiness Church Members Dead
after Taking Strychnine." The death of two martyrs for the faith
was reported. It stated that the assistant pastor and a member of a
Cocke County Holiness Church died Saturday night after they
drank strychnine in what was called a test of faith. It said that
Sheriff Bobby Stinson identified the victims as Reverend Jimmy
Ray Williams, aged thirty four of Carson Springs, and Buford
Pack, aged thirty of Marshall, North Carolina. Jimmy Williams
was assistant pastor at the Holiness Church of God in Jesus'
Name located off old Sevierville Road, known for it's practice of
handling poisonous snakes as a part of religious services. Pack was
member of the church. Sheriff Stinson reportedly said he found
Pack dead at the home located near the church of his brother

Reverend Liston Pack. Reverend Liston Pack is pastor of the holiness church. Liston Pack reportedly told sheriff Stinson that several members were having a religious meeting at the church. He is reported to have said that they had several snakes in the church and a bottle of strychnine on the altar. The snakes and strychnine were out in front of everybody and the members were told if you that if they had the spirit of the Lord then the snake wouldn't bite them and the strychnine wouldn't kill them. Sheriff Stinson is reported to have said that said Liston Pack told him that no one was forced to handle snakes or drink poison. It was reported that several members of the church handled the snakes but only Reverend Williams and Buford Pack drank an undetermined amount strychnine.

Frank Perice, who was at the services, said that Williams had 1 ounce of powder strychnine and had a pint jar and got water from the spring and mixed the strychnine in the water. Sheriff Stinson said one person who was unidentified had been bitten on the hand by a snake. Asked if he wanted medical treatment the man said the Lord would take care of his wounds. After the service began, several members of the church took out the snakes and began handling them. Reverend Williams is reported to have had a glass of water and to have poured strychnine into it. He reportedly said, "I don't know if this is strychnine, but I'm going to drink it later. Someone called Reverend Pack outside telling him that Buford was sick. He was in his car and Frank Perice was holding the light switch off as he complained that he could not stand any light. About 11:00 P.M., Reverend Liston Pack said he returned and found Buford lying on the hood of a car. They said Buford drank a gallon of water out of the spring that ran out the hollow after he drank the strychnine. When Buford died, Liston Pack carried him on his shoulder to his house nearby. Before the services were over, Pack said he saw Williams lying on the floor of the church near the pulpit. He was a laughing. Reverend Williams later drove himself to his home in his truck. He was found dead in his truck.

Reverend Pack carried him into the Williams's home. He said, "One of these men was my brother, and I've worshipped with the other for five years now." He went on to say, "I believe they felt the same way I do. If I am bitten by a snake or drink strychnine and die, I'll be that much closer to the Kingdom of God."

Funeral services were be at the Holiness Church of God in Jesus' Name. As requested by Jimmy Ray Williams before his death, 2 Timothy 3:6–8 was read: "For I am now ready to be offered, and the time of my departure is at hand. I have fought the good fight; I have finished my course; I have kept the faith. Henceforth there is laid up for me a crown of righteousness which the Lord, the righteous judge, shall give me at that day and not to me only, but unto all them also that love his appearing." Jimmy had also requested that serpents be handled at his funeral and that if anyone was anointed to, that strychnine be drunk. Reverend Alfred Ball officiated at the funeral. Jimmy was buried upon a hill not far from the church. This was in April of 1973.

Funeral services for Pack were held at his home in Route 5, Marshall, North Carolina. He was buried at the Naulty family cemetery beside the church.

Following the deaths of Williams and Pack, the law attempted to stop the Carson Springs church from handling serpents and drinking poison. In the local newspaper, an article headed "Suit Filed to Stop Church Members from Handling Snakes and Drinking Poison" reported that Attorney General Henry F. Dutch Swann filed an injunction in Cocke County Circuit Court to stop members of the Holiness Church of God in Jesus' Name from drinking poison. The attorney general was also quoted as saying he may seek an injunction against the church in connection with the deaths of the minister's brother Buford Pack and Reverend Jimmy Williams who died April 7 after drinking strychnine at church services.

After Reverend Pack was served injunction papers, he told the *Newport Plain Talk* that he planned to continue having

services, including handling snakes and drinking poison. "We try
to obey the laws of the land but God's laws come first," he said.

A hearing on the injunction was scheduled before Circuit
Judge George R. Shepherd. Named as defendants in the suit were
Drew Click, Robert Grooms, Clyde Rickerd, Alfred Ball, and
Reverend Liston Pack. All were described in the petition as
elders or members of the church. The suit noted that several
members of the church, including the late Reverend Williams
and Buford Pack as well as Liston Pack, had previously been found
guilty of handling poisonous snakes in October 1970.

Another newspaper article reported on the court's ruling
regarding the Carson Springs church. In an article headed
"Shepherd Snake Handling but Church Members Can Drink
Poison," the *Newport Plain Talk* reported that Circuit Judge
George R. Shepherd had granted a temporary injunction barring
members of Holiness Church of God in Jesus' Name from
handling snakes at services, but ruled that an individual can drink
poison as long as he doesn't offer it to someone else. The
newspaper went on to report that a large crowd jammed the
courtroom to witness the almost-friendly confrontation between
Judge Shepherd and Reverend Liston Pack, pastor of the church.
The crowd grew so large that officers were ordered to remove
people standing in the aisles and to lock the doors.

On Saturday night, over a hundred persons, including several
newsman, crowded into the tiny Carson Spring church to see if
Reverend Pack would carry out promises to take up serpents
despite the judge's orders. No snakes were handled nor poison
drunk in a two-and-a-half-hour service filled with singing
shouting, and preaching, the paper reported. In handing down the
ruling, Judge Shepherd said he would be violating his oath to
support the Constitution and the laws of the land if he allowed
snake handling to continue. He added that the law could do very
little to stop persons from drinking poison. He was reported as
saying he thought the drinking of poison would be classified as a
suicide.

The paper noted that the ruling stopped short of attorney
general Swann's contention that snake handling and poison
drinking should be permanently stopped.

Speaking of the two deaths at the Carson Springs church,
Reverend Ball was quoted as saying, "We wouldn't, we couldn't
have stopped these boys. They wanted to do this. They believed
they wouldn't be harmed."

Reverend Ball emerged as the main spokesman for the
defendants who chose to face the hearing with no attorney.
Reverend O. V. Shoupe of Canton, North Carolina, told the
court that he had been charged in Frankfort, Kentucky, in 1942
for snake handling even though there was no state law against
handling at that time. He asked to represent the defendants, but
judge Shepherd said the members could be represented only by
themselves or by an attorney.

Attorney General Swann called to Tennessee Bureau of
Criminal Identification agent Ed Ashburn and Eugene Pack, a
brother to Liston, to testify. Eugene Pack testified he had
attended services in Carson Springs on April 7 during which
Buford and Williams drank fatal doses of strychnine. He testified
that church members had taken snakes from boxes behind the
church pulpit and wrapped them around their necks hands arms.
He said an unidentified person (described as an Indian) was bitten
by a snake and that his arm had swelled. Pack went on to tell the
court told that he saw Wlliams and Pack drink from a glass on the
pulpit. He testified that Pack died thirty-five to forty minutes
later, while Williams lived two or three hours before he died.
Pack testified that both the sheriff's department and the rescue
squad tried to persuade Williams to go for medical treatment but
that Jimmy said, "God will take care of me." Eugene Pack also
testified that snakes were handled during the funeral service at
William's gravesite.

Agent Ashburn testified that Liston Pack told him that
Williams brought the strychnine to church, but Pack refused to
tell him where the strychnine was obtained. Upon taking the
stand, Eugene Pack told the court that his church's snake-

handling and poison-drinking practices were often wrongly called tests of faith. "We do not test our faith," he said. "It is a sign to confirm the Word of God to the unbelievers."

Judge Shepherd noted that Pack and other members of the church had been charged with snake handling in 1970 after snakes were taken to Sand Hill Church of God in Jesus' Name in Del Rio, Tennessee, without permission of its congregation. Judge Shepherd had found them guilty but suspended punishment. Pack stated, "You told us to get our own land and own church. We went out and bought two acres of land and got our church so we could handle snakes there."

The only other defense witness was James Brickhead, a part-time teacher of religion and anthropology at the University of Alberta in Canada. He testified he had attended services at the holiness church seventy-five times as part of a study. He testified that he never felt the snake handling endangered him. He testified that he had seen the late Reverend Williams drink carbon tetrachloride, a poisonous cleaning fluid.

Reverend Ball handed a petition in support of the church's practices to Judge Shepherd with about 200 signatures. Judge Shepherd said he could not accept it. He expressed concern over the widespread news coverage of the church's activity and asked Reverend Pack if he had invited the newsman. "No we never asked them to come but we always welcomed them," Pack said.

Attorney General Swann was reported in the local paper as stating that he might seek an involuntary manslaughter indictment against Reverend Pack in the two deaths. Judge Shepherd advised him he probably ought not to go that far supporting Reverend Ball's statement that Pack ought not be held responsible for someone else's suicide. Ball said that Buford Pack was not the boss, he was just a servant of the people. Each church member obeys the convictionof his own heart, Ball told the court.

Several newsmen attended the hearing. Judge Shepherd called members of the press into his chambers before the session and advised them that pictures could be taken in the courtroom since no jury was present, but barred pictures of himself while he was on the bench. Cameras continually clicked throughout the proceedings.

The local paper reported on May 9, 1973, that the Cocke County grand jury returned no true blll in the deaths of Pack and Williams. Reverend Pack was exonerated of involuntary manslaughter and handling poisonous snakes. One grand jury member reportedly said that the members of the grand jury did not think Reverend Pack could be charged in connection with other persons taking their own lives. This grand jury member also said the members of the grand jury did not believe that handling serpents endangered anybody other than the one handling.

Despite the grand jury's decision, church members are presently barred from handling snakes as result of order by Circuit Judge George R. Shepherd. Swann told the grand jury he would bring more charges against Pack if the order were ever violated.

The grand jury members were J. C. Holdway, Oscar Ottinger, Ermal Moore, M. O. Allen, Jr., James P. Griffen, Ronnie Smith, Tom J. Odell, James E. Frisbee, Buddy Hudd, Sr., George William Boozer, Thomas J. Good, Reverend Roe Ford, and my wife's (Pamela Ford Morrow) uncle.

Soon the local paper was reporting on the arrest of serpent-handling believers. In an article on "Snake Handling Ministers," it was reported that Sheriff Bobby Stinson escorted holiness ministers Reverend Alfred Ball and Liston Pack to Cocke County jail for not paying court fines. It reported that the two elders of the Holiness Church of God in Jesus' Name surrendered voluntarily at the sheriff's office after services at the Carson Springs church. The fines were levied after Pack and Ball were found guilty of contempt of court for violating an order banning snake handling at the church. In a statement before entering the jail, Pack reportedly said that Judge Shepherd had told them they would have thirty days to pay the fines and that their time was not yet up. When asked if he planned to pay his fine, Ball said he didn't have the money. "I've got a ten-month-old child to feed and I don't have any money for any fines," he is reported to have said.

In "Snake Handling Ministers Jailed," the newspaper reported that Liston Pack and Alfred Ball remained in Cocke County jail after Circuit Judge Shepherd ordered them jailed for not paying fines levied for contempt of court. "We're not going to pay fines, and we've got to keep on handling snakes. They might as well get used to that," Reverend Pack was quoted as saying.

Attorney General Swann said he had proof the men had handled snakes at the church since Judge Shepherd's contempt of court ruling. The judge sentenced Pack to thirty days and Ball to twenty days in jail but suspended the terms on condition that they not handle snakes at the church again.

The Newport *Plain Talk* reported that Michael Ellis, an attorney for the American Civil Liberties Union, had agreed to take Pack's case at no charge. It was reported that Ellis would file an appeal to the Tennessee Supreme Court seeking to overturn the original ruling barring snake handling during church services. Judge Shepherd ruled that the two would not be allowed to make bonds if their case was appealed.

Occasionally the papers report on church members who are found not guilty of violating the law. In one instance, the local paper reported that Drew Click was found not guilty after testimony indicated even though was a member of a serpent-handling church he had never personally handled. It reported that another defendant, Reverend Clyde Ricker, lived in North Carolina and no papers could be served on him. It noted that a third man, Jerry Wilds, was not known by either the prosecutors or the defendants; Attorney General Swann had charged all the defendants with handling serpents. Those present were not represented by an attorney. They pleaded not guilty to the charges.

Liston Pack who took the stand on his behalf reportedly said that the attorney general is going to be in lots of trouble and spending a lot of money to bring these witnesses to court. He was quoted as saying, "I admit I handle snakes. A Christian man won't lie. All you have to do is ask me." "I believe you, Pack. I believe you," Judge Shepherd answered softly. "I believe any individual should have the right to worship the dictates of his own heart," Pack said. Swann is reported to have said that he believed these to be honest people, but they must obey the law. He said the state has a right to protect people. Swann compared the case with the Mormon religion and members who practice polygamy, or having more than one wife. "That's one of the most sincere churches there is, but they still got them for violating the law," he is reported to have said.

Pack chided Swann for bringing the preachers to court, claiming he should be investigating houses of prostitution, vandals, and murders instead of wasting time with a church where people pick up serpents. Pack said he thought the snake-handling law was a good law when it applied to handling or displaying serpents that could endanger others but that did not apply to handling serpents in church. Ball told the court, "If we violate the law it's because we feel that salvation of our souls is more important."

The controversy surrounding the deaths of Williams and Pack occurred in the late summer of 1973. The Holiness Church of God in Jesus' Name continued to have services until 1992. In that year the church was destroyed by fire. After the fire, the last few members of the church were going to rebuild the church. However, it was sold to Liston Pack for the sum of one dollar. After I heard that the land was gong to be sold, I and the few remaining members of the Carson Springs church got land in Edwina and built a new church, the Edwinia Church of God in Jesus Christ's Name. This was 1993.

# Chapter 12

"But first must he suffer many things, and be rejected of this generation."(Luke 17:25)

# Trouble in the Churches:
# More Deaths and Bites

Serpent handling remains popular in Kentucky since it was first introduced in Pineville by George Hensley in 1919. It is practiced all over Eastern Kentucky and in parts of all other counties in Kentucky. At times the courts had locked the doors of churches that refused to stop handling serpents. Sizemore, a church member who had been locked out of his church, said people can't understand how it feels to be locked out of their church. "The church is where I found salvation and where I worship God in Spirit and truth. I go to a lot of other churches, but the're just not the same," he told me. "A serpent-handling church is where I want to go."

The church was founded in the early sixties under the name the Church of God the Pillar and the Ground and Truth. Within several years a faction of the congregation emerged opposed to the practice of serpent handling. George North, a trustee of the church vowed that he would put a stop to serpent handling in the Pineville church and brought a lawsuit against the church. After his death, Gladis North vowed to continue her husband's lawsuit. The church members who supported North placed a padlock on the door. Knox Circuit Judge Lewis Hopper said he would allow the lock to remain until the case was resolved.

When we were locked out of our church, inside it was just as it had been left. Guitars were propped against the wall, an advertising calendar was opened to November and the Ten Commandments were posted in black letters on a large white board. When the church was unlocked, Pastor Sizemore fell to his knees before the pulpit. He said, "I've been to other places, but there is no place like home, no place like the church where you grew up in Christian ways." Tears were welling in his eyes as he told me this. Once the bridge can be repaired, he has decided to hold services in the church again. Will they include snakes? "They will be taken in there just like nothing ever happened," Sizemore said. The small church now has about thirty active members.

Glenn Summerford had just got out of prison. He repented and was baptized in Jesus Christ's Name. He opened an old gas station and turned it in to a church. He named it the Church of Jesus. He became widely known as result of a highly-published trial in which he was convicted of attempting to murder his wife.

One newspaper ran an article headed "Snake Handling Preacher Tried to Kill His Wife." It recounted how Glenn had backslid and got out church. The paper went on to say that his wife, Darlene Summerford, said that the forty-seven-year-old Glenn wanted her dead so he could marry another woman. At the trial in Scottsboro, Darlene claimed Glenn grabbed her by the hair and dragged her to the building where he kept his snakes. She told the jury that Glenn then took a pipe and hit the cage real hard to get the snakes real mad. Then Darlene claimed Glenn grabbed her by the hair again and said he would push her face in the snake box if she didn't stick her hand in the snake box. Darlene then testified that she put her hand in the snake box and was immediately bit twice in rapid succession. She also that Glenn said she had to die because he wanted to marry another woman.

Darlene recovered from he rattlesnake bites at a local hospital. She had been married to Glenn for sixteen years. They have ten children from their current and previous marriages,

Church members say they fought regularly over the past years. Tension between the couple reached a peak during the month before the rattlesnake bite in the fall of 1991. "It was a week of pure hell," Darlene said.

Glenn Summerford countered his wife's accusations of infidelity and attempted murder with similar charges. Glenn said Darlene was dating another preacher and that she had tried to kill Glenn months earlier with one of his own serpents.

At the trial, Tammy Flippo, a twenty-three-year-old member of Glenn's church testified that she had witness Darlene actually try to kill Glenn. She testified that Darlene got Glenn so drunk that he passed out. She then went outside to the snake building to get a snake to put on him, but it bit Darlene instead.

Under cross-examination, Tammy said she never dated Summerford or had any social relationship with Glenn other than attending services. Glenn, who served time in prison before on two separate felony convictions, risked coming under Alabama's "three strike rule."

The church raised money to post a $20,000 bond so that Glenn could be released from jail pending an appeal of his case. His appeal failed and the "three-strike" rule in Alabama applied. Under this rule, a third felony coviction carries essentially a life sentence. Glenn was sentenced to ninety-nine years in prison where he remains today.

A newspaper in Bridgeport, Alabama, reported that a church-goer survived snakebite. Ruble Garner of Bridgeport, Alabama, had been handling poisonous snakes for fifty-three years before he was bitten for the first time. Garner, aged seventy-nine, was holding two copperheads during a religious service at the Rock House Holiness Church in the Macedonia community near Section, Alabama, when one bit him on the right hand just below the thumb. "I must have not been under the anointing enough," Garner said at home while holding an ice pack on the swollen right hand. Garner refused medical attention, even after paramedics arrived at the church. He said someone in the congregation had called for an ambulance right away after he was bitten.

Garner is a former pastor of a serpent-handling church he built here thirty-four years ago. Garner said he trusted Jesus to heal him. "If you're going to take them up, you ought to trust in the Lord," he said. Garner said the snake that bit him also had bitten two others on two separate occasions. After he was bitten, Garner said he placed both serpents in a box and resumed praying with the other church members. Although he said he felt the bite, he was never in any pain. "Even now, it doesn't hurt," said Garner as he moved the ice pack to reveal two puncture wounds. "The Lord's healing power is the only thing I know that can explain why it doesn't hurt."

Reverend Billy Summerford is pastor of the Rock House Holiness Church. He said the decision to seek help after a bite is up to the individual.

Newspapers reported that Reverend Gerald Fleenor was in guarded condition at the University of Tennessee hospital after being bitten by a snake at a church service. Members of his Sneedville Holiness Church stated he would not be in the hospital if his mother had more faith in the Bible.

Fleenor was bitten on a Sunday afternoon while he was handling a rattlesnake while attending a church service at the Ages Pentecostal holiness Church in Harlan, Kentucky, where Gray Long is pastor. After Fleenor returned to Sneedville his mother reportedly insisted that he be checked by a doctor. Darlene Smith, a Sneedville Holiness Church member, stated that if Gerald's mother had more faith he would have been all right. Smith went on to say that Fleenor was bitten about 2:00 P.M. A Holiness minister from Virginia, Austin Long, drove him home shortly afterwards. He then called his mother who contacted the Hancock County rescue squad. Fleenors mother is not a member of the holiness church. It was reported that Fleenor had been handing serpents for a little over a year before receiving this, his first, bite.

Newspapers reported that rattlesnakes at the same church bit two men within a three-month period in Harlan, Kentucky. The earlier victim got medical attention and lived; the last victim did not and died. Harlan County Coroner William Venable stated that Earnest W. Short, aged forty-one, of Teetersville died at his father's home. He did not seek medical treatment for a rattlesnake bite he received during a church service. Short was bitten at the Ages Pentecostal Church. The pastor, Gary Long Venable, said the church is located between Harlan and Evarts, Kentucky.

Reverend Gerald Fleenor, aged twenty-nine of Sneedville, was bitten in November at the same church. Under Kentucky law handling snakes during religious services is a misdemeanor punishable by a fine of $50 to $100. However charges are rarely brought against church members who handle serpents. Serpent handling is a regular practice in many churches throughout the mountains of Appalachia today and it will continue to be despite the law.

Previous to Short's death, the last known death from a snakebite during a church service occurred in Harlan County on February 13, 1986. Newspapers regularly report that members of some strict fundamentalist Church of God churches believe the Bible directs them to handle poisonous snakes as evidence of their faith in Christ.

Newspapers reported that an Ohio man was in a Lexington hospital after being bitten by a snake during a church service in Leslie County. It was reported that state police said Turman Frye, about forty-three, of Springfield was listed in fair condition in the intensive care unit at the University of Kentucky Albert B. Chandler Medical Center. A rattlesnake bit Frye on the hand during a service at Grassy Pentecostal Church at Stinnett, Kentucky. Frye was first taken to Breckinridge Hospital in Hyden and then transferred to the University of Kentucky hospital. State police reportedly said they could not say yet if charges would be filed.

Newspapers in Georgia reported that a man died after being bitten by a snake at church service in Cartersville. He was bitten on the jaw while handling a rattlesnake during a religious service. He was taken to Humana Hospital. Nursing Supervisor Gail Deckard said Arnold Lee Loveless, aged forty-eight, died at 11:20 P.M. Monday from the bite he received Sunday at the Church of Jesus Christ near Rome. Bartow County Sheriff Don Thurman reportedly said the snake was taken to the hospital so doctors could determine the correct remedy. Then the snake was taken to an animal shelter. Thurman said the snake was returned to the church at the request of a member of the congregation. Sheriff's department reports said Mr. Loveless removed a copperhead from a wooden crate and began praying over it. As he removed a rattlesnake from the same crate it bit him on the jaw. Witnesses were rooted as saying Loveless began to pray and that fellow worshipper laid hands on him in an attempt to heal the bite. They said emergency medical workers were not notified until Loveless became violently ill.

Darrell Fee of Rose Hill, aged forty-five, died after being bitten at a church near Lafollette, Tennessee. Newspapers reported that the Campbell County Sheriff's Department was investigating the death that occurred on August 29, 2000. Captain Scott Amish was reported to have said that Darrell died. In Virginia after being bitten during a service at the Ivy Bell Church of God. on Sunday, August 27. He said that he understood that Darrell was handling black timber rattler snake when it bit him on the chest. He chose not to seek medical attention. He didn't want the bite reported to authorities. A Virginia medical examiner confirmed that the cause of death was the bite to Darell's chest. He was reported to have said that about thirty to forty people were in attendance at the church, but most of them just didn't want to say much about what had happened.

Newspapers reported that a Bell County man of a snakebite he suffered during a religious service at Pine Mountain in the Arjay Community of Bell County, Kentucky. The man was Daril R Collins, aged twenty-three. It was reported that the Kentucky state police in Harlan said District Judge James Bowling signed an order at midnight requiring medical treatment for Collins. The county commonwealth's attorney Karen Blondell was reported to have said that someone at the home had called for an ambulance Sunday. However, when emergency officials arrived, Collins could not talk, his pupils were dilated and his arm was severely swollen and he was unable to give consent to medical treatment, Bowling reportedly said. Officials asked Collins wife to consent for him but she refused. State police were summoned, but they were also denied permission to take Collins, Trooper Don Perry was reported as saying. By the time emergency officials returned to the home with a court order, Collins was already dead.

In an earlier case Bowling refused to sign an arrest warrant against a minister of a serpent-handling church after a member died from a bite. Bowling said this situation was different because it was still possible legally to save Collin's life. He is reported to have compared Collin's situation to a person who has a gunshot wound. If the person is unable to give consent, the court has jurisdiction to require medical treatment.

The Collins funeral service was held at Saylor Pentecostal Church in Crockett, Kentucky. This is where another man died from a serpent bite received during a service in 1995. The Arnett & Steele funeral home in Pineville was in charge of funeral arrangements. No changes were ever filed in the death of Collins.

In the *Lexington Herald-Leader* on Wednesday, December 17, 1997, there appeared an article headed "Mountain Preacher's Death Reopens Serpent-Handling Debate." It stated that on Friday, March 10, 1995, state police were investigating the death of a mountain preacher Kale Saylor, who was bitten by a rattlesnake. It said that Saylor's death has reopened discussion of the Appalachian religious practice of snake handling, which was outlawed in Kentucky in 1942. Saylor, of Bledsoe in Southeastern Kentucky, died around 1:30 A.M. Wednesday at the Pineville community hospital, according to Clay Howard of the Mount

Pleasant funeral home. Neither Howard nor hospital officials would release a cause of death.

Saylor was minister at a Pentecostal church that bears his name at Stoney Fork, just across the line in Bell County. The incident allegedly occurred Sunday, Trooper Johnny Collins of the state police post in Harlan said it was unclear whether it was during a religious ceremony. Bell county deputy coroner Bill Bisceglia said his office was not notified. Collins said state police did not find out about the death until late Wednesday. Two of Saylor's sons, Kale Saylor, Jr., and Stratton Saylor, declined to comment.

A newspaper reported that Ruth Farler of Perry County, Kentucky, tried to get authorities to crack down on the practice of serpent handling last year after a snake bit her son, Virgil Gibson, at a Leslie County church. He spent several days in the hospital. "It's so sad," she reportedly said when told of Saylor's death. "They will just keep on handling them, of course." She expressed concern that the police seem to do nothing about it.

Saylor's death is not seen by other devotees as an indictment of snake handling or as a weakening of Saylor's faith. People simply believe this was God's way of calling Saylor home. Probably, if anything, it makes them believe that much stronger.

In recent years one of the most publicized deaths from serpent bite was that of Melinda Brown whose husband would suffer the same fate just three years late. In a newspaper article headed "Victim of Snake Bite Eulogized As Willing to Die for Her Faith," it was reported that Melinda Brown was bitten by a rattlesnake Sunday in a Middlesboro, Kentucky, church. She refused medical aid and died Tuesday. A black rattlesnake she had taken from her husband, John Brown, Jr., fatally bit her, widely know as "Punkin" Brown. The snake was across her left arm and sank its fangs into her just below her left elbow. The bite occurred at a homecoming service in August of 1995. She was twenty-eight years old and the mother of five children.

Jimmy Ray Williams was also twenty-eight years old when he died after being bitten once on the wrist by a black timber rattlesnake during a service at the House of Prayer in Jesus' Name on Sawyer Road and Roe junction near the Witt community of Hamblen County in Morristown, Tennessee.

At the Rock House Holiness Church, on a Saturday night, John Wayne "Punkin" Brown, Jr., died within an hour of being bitten by one of the rattlesnake he so often used to demonstrate his religious faith. Punkin Brown was thirty-four when he died.

A copperhead bit Darrel Phillips on the hand May of 2001. Pastor Jamie Coots was bitten on top of the head by a rattlesnake in a church service in Mibblesboro, Kentucky, in May 2001.

Roscoe Mullins, Jr., was bitten in the belly by a rattlesnake as he was putting it back in the box. He was bit at the House of Prayer in Jesus' Name in Kentucky in July 2001.

A newspaper article headed "Snake Bite Victim in Serious Condition" reported that a Huntington man remained in serious condition Monday night at Park View Memorial Hospital after bitten by a black rattlesnake during church ceremonies Sunday. About eleven in the morning, a timber rattler that came from the Hi-Way Holiness Church of God in Riverhaven, Tennessee, bit Roy W. Vestal, aged thirty-four. Friends reportedly rushed him to Parkview, where an anti-venom was administered. He was reportedly having trouble breathing, was going into shock, and showed signs of internal bleeding when he arrived at the hospital, spokesman Jim Tobalski said. Vestal was the first snakebite victim treated at Parkview this year. Tobalski said because Parkview is a regional trauma center it must keep a certain amount of anti-venom in supply; Tobaslski said poisonous snake bites are not that common in Northwest Indiana, which means the hospital can't store too much anti-venom. Like any other medication or drug, Tobalski said, it has an expiration date. Snake venom contains hemotoxins, which attack the blood vessels and cause swelling and hemorrhaging, and neurotoxins, which attack the nervous system and other vital organs. Neurotoxins can cause death through suffocation or heart failure after administering the anti-venom.

Roy W. Vestal also was bitten August 26, 2001, at his house and he was taken to the hospital. He told me his little fingers was rotting off where the snake bit him three weeks ago. He told me he would lose it from the bite.

The *Harlan Daily Enterprise* reported that an Ohio woman died in Harlan County after being by an eastern diamond back rattlesnake during a wake service for her uncle. State police said Shirley McLeary, aged thirty-eight of Toledo, was bitten on the arm while handling an eastern diamond back rattlesnake about 10:00 P.M. The bite occurred at the Church of the Lord Jesus Christ in Baxter, in Harlan County. Ms. McLeary had been attending a wake for her uncle, Marion Rowe, aged eighty-six. Marion was a bishop in the church. Ms McLeary is Pete Rowe's sister, reached by telephone, Dorothy Toney, a daughter of Marion Rowe and a cousin of Ms. McLeary, said what happened was the will of God. It wasn't her will. She reportedly declined to discuss the incident further.

The same paper reported that a long-time funeral director in Harlan County who declined to be identified said he had performed funerals for about ten people bitten during such services in his forty years. Authorities did not recover the snake that delivered the fatal bite. They reportedly said they did not know how many snakes were used in the service or who was responsible for them.

What I was told happened at the church was that a wake was being held for Marion Rowe. They brought his body to the church and a member of the church that handled serpents said the feeling was just not right that night. Another person told me that the serpents were already at the church when he got to the wake. One serpent was a large eastern diamond back rattlesnake that came from out of the mountains of West Virginia. Another member said that Shirley reached into the box, got the serpent out, and was handling it over the coffin of her uncle. She had the serpent in her hand with her arm in the air when it bit her. She was taken to a house next door where she died about 5:15

Thursday morning, after she was bitten Wednesday night. No charges were filed in her death.

Silas Crawford was in Middlesboro at Pastor Jamie Coot's church for a service. He come down from Ohio. When Silas got there, he was down and out. He had the church members to pray for him. Then he went to the serpent boxes and got four Northern copperheads and one Southern copperhead out of the boxes and was handling all of them at once. All five copperheads bit him. In a few seconds, he could not breath. He was carried out of the church by Jason Barnes and Daniel to the pastor Jamie Coot's house. His hand was swollen to twice its normal size. This was March of 2001. In the third week in August 1999 at the High Way Holiness Church of God, Silas was twice bitten on the chest by a broad-banded copperhead form Texas. His chest turned black and blue. This was Aronald Saylor's Church in Indianapolis, Indiana.

Jason Barnes was bitten twice at the Faith Tabernacle in Jesus' Name in Middlesboro, Kentucky—once in 1999 and again in 2000. Both bites were by copperheads.

Jamie Coots was bitten at the funeral of Ray MaCallester, a longtime serpent handler who died a natural death.

Dewey Chafin is a well-known serpent handler who has been bitten hundreds of times. In the summer of 2001, he was bit by a 52-inch Southern copperhead. He had a section of his hand rotted out from the bite, Dewey has never received medical attention for any of his bites.

# Chapter 13

"Let a man so account of us, as of the ministers of Christ, and stewards of the mysteries of God. Moreover it is required in stewards. That a man be found faithful." (1 Corinthians 4:1–2)

# The Del Rio and Edwina Churches of God in Jesus Christ's Name

In 1978 I met Pamela Ford. We dated a few months and got married July 8 at Sister Mary Turner's house up on Flat Branch. Her son Marvin Turner did the marriage service. We lived in the old 15th six years at the old Mary Cagle place across from Timman Ball's old store on the other side of the creek. We then lived two years in Chapel Hollow in old Click House on the old Christy mission site.

In June of 1986, the Lord blessed my wife and me with a piece of ground in slab town in Del Rio, Tennessee (now call Blue-Mill). Pam's uncle Frank Pierce died in 1999. Tommy Coots, the pastor the Middlesboro Church of the Lord Jesus Christ, preached his funeral service at the church. Rayford Dunn, John Brown, Pam, and I went together to Kentucky to his funeral.

At the funeral they asked the brothers to testify. They took turns preaching and testifying after that part of the service that had singing. All the people came up front of the church and to pay their last respects before the closing of the coffin.

After the funeral we left for Newport, Tennessee, and then to Del Rio where we live. During the week I would work at odd jobs. I also painted and helped build houses. The time I was not working for other people Pam and I were working on our cabin.

In the same year (1986), Pam and I went to several churches around and about. I had an appointment to preach in Marshal, North Carolina, once a month at the House of Prayer in Jesus Christ's Name. I also preached at the Holiness Church of God in Jesus' Name at Carson Springs, near Newport, Tennessee, and at the Sand Hill Church of God in Jesus' Name in Del Rio. Pam and I also went to the House of Prayer in Jesus' Name on Fridays where I preached some. We also went to services once a month at Thomson Branch. If the Lord gave us victory, we would take up serpents.

At that time serpent handling was going on in every service. Today in 2003 you don't see as much serpent handling. Not as many people carry serpents to church or hunt serpents as was common in the past. Still, the tradition continues.

In January of 1987, Pam and I moved out of the Old 15th and into our cabin in slab town in Del Rio. We got settled down. At about the same time, they closed the church in Marshal, North Carolina. It was not reopened until 1995.

I was preaching at two churches at Morristown and in the hollow at Liston Pack's church where he was the pastor. In October of that that year, I had my serpents in the car and Liston came out and told me, "You can't bring serpents in this church anymore." Liston Pack told people that serpents would not be in the Holiness Church of God in Jesus' Name anymore. As far as I know, no more serpents were in the church from that time on until it burnt down in 1992.

We also had lots of prayer meeting around and about the Del Rio community where we live. In August I started a small church that was only 16 by 30 feet. I named the church the Del Rio Church of God in Jesus' Name. I built onto it as I could. My daddy-in-law, John Ike Ford helped when he could. He was a real fine man. In the eleven years that I knew him, I never heard him say a harmful word about anyone. He died in 1989 on the first Sunday after Passover. Every Passover lilies are blooming and the grass is turning green. Everything that was asleep during the winter months starts to wake up. You know in your heart that one day soon Jesus Christ is coming back to resurrect his saints out of their sleep and they will live forever and ever with him.

During the summer of 1987, I finished the rest of the cabin. I put gutters on it and stained the cabin cedar brown. In the winter months, I worked on the small church. I got it finished in the spring of 1988. We had the first service in it. We had the Passover and the Lord's supper and foot washing.

The Jesus' Name believers have witnessed the power of God over and over again. Many people find it hard to believe what we have seen Jesus do in our lives. He gives us power to cast out demons and to raise the dead. Here are some examples I want to share with you.

Charles told me that he lived on Big Creek. He and his wife, Christy, went to a Holiness Church of God at Stone Mountain. Brain Gregg was the pastor at the time. A woman prophetess was at the meeting. There was a sickly young man that who could not eat or sleep. He was tormented all the time. The woman had the discerning of spirits. She told the young man, Rodie, to come forth. She told him he had a sickly devil in him. This sickly devil made him sick all the time and tormented him. She laid hands on Rodie and told him that the Word of God says they shall cast out devils. She said, "I cast you out in the name of Jesus." Rodie fell to the floor. Charles said that he was sitting on the third bench. He saw the boy was laying on the floor. Charles saw a foam mass of very small bubbles come out of Rodie's mouth. The he saw a mist. Charles said he was the only that could see it or hear sounds. The mist came out of Rodie's mouth. It turned into an image that was half bat and half rat. It was reddish and pinkish in color. It jumped on the pulpit and looked at the pastor and at the woman prophetess. It then looked at the young man he had just come out of. It turned on the pulpit and saw Brian and the woman prophetess praising the Lord. The devil turned and looked at Charles. It hollered loud sounds, then made a loud scream. Charles said the scream was a loud sharp piercing cry. It frightened him and sent cold chills down his spine. The hairs on his arms began to rise up on end. The devil stared right at him. It then flew off the pulpit. It flew straight at him. He saw it coming and felt a dread. As it was coming toward him he put his hand over his mouth. He felt the devil land on his face and try to go into his mouth and down his throat. He felt it crawl over his nose and then up into his nose hole and down his throat. Charles told me he has been sickly ever since. He told me he needs the demon cast out of him or he will always be sickly.

Also, years ago Brother Perry Bettis left his house in Dolly Pond to preach at a service at a Jesus' Name Church somewhere in the west Tennessee hills When he got to the church, it was full. There was a man that had a demon in him. He started to run all around the church. He was knocking people down and striking at others. The demon-possessed man's tongue was hanging out 6 inches long. Saliva was spewing from his mouth. He started up to the pulpit where Perry was preaching. Brother Perry took hold of the man and threw him to the floor. Perry startled the man, holding him down while he asked the members to come and help him to pray. The demon-possessed man's tongue was still hanging out as it began to swell. It was getting larger and thicker. It got so big it could not go back into the man's mouth. Perry and the members kept praying and asking Jesus Christ to cast the demon out. The demon finally left, and the swelling in the tongue started going down. After a while the man was okay—the demon was cast out.

Another time, back in the 1950s, Perry Bettis and Tom Harden were having a brush harbor meeting. A large number of people were gathered at the meeting. A wicked man and his wife also were there. While Brother Tom was preaching the gospel of Jesus Christ with the signs following the believers, the wicked man's wife went forward to the handmade altar to repent. The wicked man started to call Tom all kinds of dirty names. The man's action was unclean and his speech was getting dirtier. Brother Perry got the wicked man and took him outside the brush harbor; he told him not to use dirty talk against the Word of God or to use dirty speech against those who preach God's word. The wicked man said that he did not care and that he did not want his wife to repent. The man left. Perry followed him, all the time asking him to repent of his sin and to come to the Lord. The wicked man insisted that he did not want to repent. Perry stopped and the man went on his way. Perry said it was a clear night with a full moon.

The light of the moon shown on the wicked man as he was walked up the road. Perry said he saw a black shadow of a man come out of the wicked man. The shadow vanished. The wicked man, he died a sinner man. That brush arbor meeting, it was the wicked man's last altar call. The man refused the Lord and would not repent. So he died a lost man.

This is a true story that happened at a church somewhere in the mountains of North Carolina. My wife and I went to this church in April of 1980 for the Wednesday night service. It was about a quarter past seven when we arrived. The church was packed that night. I noticed there was a man there I did not know. The Lord revealed to me that he was a false prophet and had been involved in witchcraft and something bad was going to happen that night. The pastor had a singer lead off the service with singing, then he prayed and started preaching. The pastor asked the man (the false prophet) if he wanted to preach—this was his first night there at the church. He went up to the pulpit without a Bible. When he started to preach he made the strangest sound I have ever heard in my life—it made fear run all through my body. I told Pam to keep her mind upon Jesus Christ, that something bad was going to happen. When he was through preaching he asked for someone to come up and let him pray for them. No one made a move to go, then suddenly a woman jumped up and said something had been troubling her. She went up front and the false prophet laid his hand on her. Something strange started to happen—some kind of force had gotten hold of the woman. She started moving backward. It is something I will never forget as long as I live. She moved backwards past the congregation and when she got close to the door, it flew open.

Something invisible picked the woman up and threw her about twelve feet straight up into the air—when she came down she landed on some cars in the parking lot. Her head, neck, and chest hurt real badly. When she came to she was saying, "Get this big, black demon off me." She kept saying it over and over. Finally she said she didn't know what happened or how she got to church that night. Finally the false prophet left. Paul said in 2 Corinthians 11:14–15, "And no marvel, for Satan himself is transformed into an angel of light. Therefore it is no great thing if his ministers also be transformed as the ministers of righteousness, whose end shall be according to their works."

After the false prophet left, I have never seen him again. The woman's brother took her home and went back to the pastor's house. He asked the pastor what happened and the pastor said he didn't know. The woman's brother told the pastor that it was not of the Lord. The pastor replied, "You're right. I see the face of the false prophet—he's got two horns on his head." The woman got set free when a true prophet of God laid his hands on her and told the demon to leave the woman in the name of Jesus Christ. She got victory over it and is doing fine today.

Another time, back in the early fifties, a man was possessed with a demon that was trying to get the man to kill himself. Five or six of his brothers from the church went to his house and prayed that Jesus Christ would cast it out. They laid hands on the man, praying, telling the demon to leave in the name of Jesus Christ. One brother had his hands in the air as the demon left the man's body and the demon bit him. It looked like a serpent bite and it did hurt him, but the brother recovered.

Back in the early eighties a woman had a demon in her at a church. She laid down on the floor and was hitting her head, the demon was trying to kill the woman. So I went up and laid hands on her head and told the demon to leave in the name of Jesus Christ. The woman passed out as the demon left her. When she came to, she got up and said the demon was gone.

These are healings told in Ireta's own words. I remember the first miracle I saw. I was six and a half years old. My mother and I were at a Pentecostal meeting held in a house. The preacher was singing, and he got the spirit, the way Pentecostals do when they sing. It was winter, and there was a big round stove in the middle of the room. I saw him reach into the stove, still singing and giving little shouts, and he took out this big chunk of coal that had burned down to a red-hot cinder. He held it up with both hands carrying it around in the room and giving those little triumphant shouts and singing, too. All this time the others were singing and shouting and dancing around him. After the meeting, everybody kept looking at his hands to see if they were burned. There wasn't a mark on them and this was only one of the signs of this Pentecostal churches in Kentucky that mother gone to. They believed in the 16th chapter of Mark beginning with the 17th verse, where it talked about speaking in tongues, healing the sick, talking in tongues, taking up serpents, and drinking poison. These verses are in the oldest manuscripts of the Bible. When you see them happen, it makes you feel like, well God has to be in a church that can perform these signs. I was baptized when I was twelve, in 1953. I learned to play the guitar and accompany groups singing at the meetings. I felt that it was part of my serving God. It is by this singing that Pentecostals get the spirit. When I got the spirit and spoke in tongues, I didn't know what I was saying, but it was a good feeling. I never handled snakes myself. I remember one weekend I visited the church in Kentucky where I used to attend. A visiting preacher got the spirit and pulled a big rattlesnake out of the snake box he had brought with him. He twirled it around his hand and was crying out. I was on the stage behind him with the singers. I remember seeing blood start oozing out from between his fingers. Then the preacher that I seen handling fire years earlier got the spirit, and he came up and took the snake out of the other preacher's hand. He put it back in the box. The man who got bit never got sick.

When I was nineteen, I married a young man who was supposed to have been saved. One time I saw him handle snakes. I remember praying all the time. I was a Pentecostal; this is the only religion that I know. We had moved to Cincinnati in 1962. A long-time friend had married my uncle. Her name was Olene. She was an excellent singer. We went to Pentecostal meetings together and sang in different churches. Olene was also the daughter of the preacher who had handled the fire.

I was healed twice. The first was when I had a miscarriage and was hemorrhaging. In spite of this, I went to the Pentecostal meeting. I was so weak I was afraid I was going to have to leave. Then I heard Olene and her father start to sing. They got the spirit. They came and laid their hands on me. I immediately became unconscious. When I came to I felt fine, no more hemorrhaging.

The second time I got healed was when I had a gum disease. I'd worn false teeth since I was fifteen. Now years later, my mouth started swelling under my upper plate. I went about three months without my teeth and was on liquid food. I become desperate and went to a medical doctor. He looked at my mouth. He said, "You don't need me; you need an oral surgeon." He named the disease, papillomatosis, and recommended a dentist. I never went.

Olene and I were on our way to the church in Kentucky. I was singing, getting very deep into the spirit. Olene laid her hands on me. I blacked out and sank to the floor. After I came to, I spit out pieces of what seemed like dry, chewed up meat. By the time I got home I could put my false teeth in. I've never had any trouble since.

A little baby died of the flu. The parents laid the baby on the bed. Friends and relatives checked the baby to be sure it was already dead. The parents had someone get Luther Morrow. Luther was a man of the Lord and a great preacher of the gospel. When he got there, the parents, friends, and relatives were crying. They said it was too late, the baby was dead. Luther said, "It is never to late for the Lord." Luther asked the parents if they loved the Lord. The parents said they loved the Lord and vowed that they would serve the Lord. After hearing that, Luther got the baby off the bed and raises it up above his head. He said, "In the name of Jesus Christ let the life from the Lord come back into this baby." He handed the baby to the parents. What joy it was! The baby had been raised from the dead.

In the 1950s Oscar Pelfery come from Big Stone Gap, Virginia, to Tennessee to hold services at the Sand Hill Church of God in Jesus' Name. He stayed with Gill and Mary Turner. They lived about 5 miles from the church, back in a hollow called Flat Creek. It was the last house in the hollow. It set off the road just a bit. On Saturday, Oscar and Marvin were walking to church. Oscar stopped and said to Marvin, "I feel serpents are around us." About that time, a big copperhead crawled out of the weeds into the road. The power of the Holy Ghost moved on Oscar to pick up the copperhead. He reached down with his hand and took up the copperhead in the name of Jesus Christ. Oscar then turned it loose. The copperhead crawled off the other side of the road into the high weeds. Oscar told Marvin that it took the real power of God to handle serpents.

The first time Brother Perry Bettis took part in the signs of the gospel was at a church in Alabama. The church was named the Straight Creek Church of God. Tom Harden and Perry left Dolly Pond where they lived to attend the Straight Creek church. When they got to Alabama, Tom and Perry went on into the church. The service got started at 7:30. The pastor had a rule that all believers had to stay up front behind a rope that was stretched across the room in front of the church. No sinners or children were allowed up front. Only the believers were allowed to partake in the signs of the gospel. Tom and Perry went up front behind the rope. The musicians where playing their instruments and singing. The pastor was anointed and opened the serpent box. He reached into the box and got a large black rattlesnake out. He handled the serpent and then handed it to Brother Perry. Perry had good victory over the serpent and handled it for a long time. The pastor took the serpent from Perry and put it back into the box. As the anointing moved on Brother Tom Harden, he got the serpent back out. He handled it in the name of Jesus Christ. Brother Perry then reached out his hand and Tom gave him the serpent. Perry handle it again for a long while. Finally the rattler was put back in the box. And after the service, the pastor gave the rattlesnake to Tom and Perry. They left Alabama to go back to their home in Tennessee.

# Chapter 14

"And we know that all things work together for good to them that love God, to them that are called according to his purpose." (Romans 8:28)

## The Death of Jimmy Ray Williams Jr.

The first time that I meet Jimmy Ray was back in 1975. At that time I was not living right. Jimmy Ray Williams, Sr., was the pastor at the church in Carson Springs in a hollow near Newport, Tennessee. His church was called the Holiness Church of God in Jesus' Name. One Saturday night meeting, he got bit on the hand by a big copperhead. He had to stay in bed a few days. On Wednesday, some of his members that went to the church asked if I would go with them to Jimmy Williams's house in the Carson Spring community. When we got there Lester Raines got out of the truck and I got out on the other side. We went on into the house and entered the bedroom where Jimmy Williams, Sr., was lying with his hand all swollen up. This was the first time that I had seem anybody serpent bit. Other church members were there. They were praying for Jimmy. I went in the living room where I saw Jimmy Ray Williams, Jr. He had a jar with a small non-poisonous water snake. I had never been to a church that handled serpents. However, there was a serpent-handling church about 5 miles down from where I lived. The church was named the Sand Hill Church of God in Jesus' Name. They handled serpents about every week at this church.

As the year went by, I was still not living right. In October of 1975, there was a revival going on. I went on Saturday night. I

went to the altar and repented of my sins. I have been serving
the Lord Jesus Christ ever since.

I started going to the Sand Hill Church of God in Jesus'
Name at Newport where Reverend Liston Pack was the pastor. I
went to the church for ten years or more. Over the years I got to
know Jimmy Ray Williams, Jr., real good. He was a real friend.

At times when we were not working we would hunt serpents
together. Pam and I and Jimmy Ray and his wife, Teresa, would
take us a picnic dinner. After a long hunt, we would sit by a creek
and have dinner at the foot of Halls Top Mountain.

At that time Jimmy Ray lived at Carson Springs right down
below the church. There was no work in Cocke County. So
Jimmy Ray and his family took up roots and moved to Spring
Creek, North Carolina, where he got a job in construction. He
worked long hours. He would get up at four in the morning and
drive to work. It would be five or six in the evening when he got
back in from work.

Jimmy Ray bought him some land with a house trailer on it.
On weekends he would go to church over in Morristown,
Tennessee, where Bud Gregg was the pastor. He still is. The
church is called the House of Prayer in Jesus' Name. Jimmy Ray
was hard working. He was a good husband and father to his family.
He always took his family to church.

Jimmy Ray died on Saturday night, July 13, 1991. I got to the
House of Prayer in Jesus' Name early. Something had been
bothering Jimmy Ray for about eight months. He would come to
the house were I lived in Del Rio. He told me that if the Lord
didn't move on him he wanted to die and go to be with the Lord.
He did not want to backslide and die and go to hell. Service after
service that he was in you could tell that he was troubled. We
talked about the things he was going through. He told me never
to tell anybody. I told him that I would never tell. The story he
told me will go to the grave with me. I will tell no one.

Jimmy Ray wanted to be buried by his father at the
cemetery above the Holiness Church of God in Jesus' Name on
the hill where his father, Jimmy Williams, Sr., was laid to rest

eighteen years earlier. Jimmy Ray seemed to know that he did not
have long to live on this earth just as his father knew that he did
not have long to live before his death. Jimmy Williams, Sr., told
Brother Ball in 1969 that he had only five years to live or preach.
He was dead in 1973.

The service that night started at about seven thirty in the
evening. Jimmy Ray was not there when the service got started.
He and his wife Teresa got to the church about ten minutes after
services started. He shook my hand and set down. Allen, Jimmy
Ray's brother, opened the serpent box. He got a black rattlesnake
out. It was as black as coal. About that time, Adam Campbell and
J. Parton came in the church and set down. John Fish opened a
snake box and got out a big copperhead. He handled it. Terry took
the copperhead from John and then got the rattlesnake from
Allen. Terry was a dancing with the two serpents. He danced
back and forth behind the pulpit. While Allen was dancing, John
Fish took the rattlesnake back from Terry. Then Allen reached
and got the rattlesnake back from John Fish and tried to put it
back in the box. The serpent turned around and crawled out of
the box. Everytime Allen tried to get the snake in the box, the
faster it would crawl out of the box. Allen had a worried look on
his face as he tried one more time to get the rattlesnake back in
the box. Once again the snake crawled back out. I think Jimmy
Ray was thinking it was going to bite his brother; Jimmy Ray
stepped forward and reached to get the rattlesnake as it came out
of the box. While he was grasping the snake in his right hand, it
pulled its head back about 6 inches and in a lighting flash it bit
Jimmy Ray above his hand. The rattlesnake's fangs were
imbedded in his wrist. He took his left hand and tried to pull the
serpent's head back. He had to pull it a few times. You could see
the flesh on his arm pull up as the serpent's fangs were coming
out of his arm. Blood ran down his hand onto the floor. I was 4
foot in front of Jimmy Ray when he was bit. The snake seemed
like it knew it was going to bite someone before going back into
the box.

Jimmy Ray knew this was the last service that he would be in. The look on his face was long and narrow. I will never forget it. He looked around at everyone in the church. Adam and Parton got up and left. Jimmy Ray turned real pale as if his heart was failing and blood was no longer pumping in his body. He walked out of the church. He managed to get to his car and set down on the front seat beside his wife. The last words that Jimmy Ray said were "It has been a long time since I hurt this way."

Back in the early eighties Robert Grooms and I pastored the Holiness Church of God in Jesus' Name. We had a homecoming. On the Saturday night before the homecoming, we were having service. Marvin Gregg carried two copperheads into the church. One bit Jimmy Ray that night in the palm of his hand. It bit so hard it broke a fang off. Brother Gene pulled it out of Jimmy Ray's hand. The hand stayed swollen for three weeks.

This time the bite to Jimmy Ray's wrist would kill him. Allen said they should take Jimmy Ray to someone's house. John Fish told them to take him to his house in Whitepine. Allen said that before they got to the highway, Jimmy Ray's eyes started to set in his head. Teresa shook him and he come back to.

At Fish's house, Jimmy Ray started getting sicker. Somebody called 911. First to arrive at the house was a fire truck. They tried to revive Jimmy Ray. Allen said Jimmy Ray was sitting in the bathroom. He fell to the floor with a gurgling sound as his life went out of him.

The last time I saw Jimmy Ray, he was lying dead on the floor. They loaded him up on a stretcher and took him in an ambulance. He was pronounced dead on arrival at Jefferson Memorial Hospital a few hours later. Jimmy Ray had said he did not want to be taken to the hospital or the doctor.

One year before Jimmy Ray's death, I was working at his house. We were building a room and a back porch onto his trailer. That night his wife said one thing that I will never forget as long as I live. Teresa told Jimmy Ray that his daughter, Susie, was going to be eleven years old on her birthday. She told Jimmy Ray that he was also eleven years old when Jimmy Williams, Sr., died in the signs of the gospel. Just as his daddy died when Jimmy Ray was eleven years old, Teresa said Jimmy Ray would be dead in the signs of the gospel when Susie turns eleven years old. After Susie's eleventh birthday, Jimmy Ray was bitten by the rattlesnake and died in the signs of the gospel at the House of Prayer in Jesus' Name in Morristown, Tennessee, on a Saturday night, July 13, 1991.

I wish I had as much faith as Jimmy Ray. A man who never knew him stopped by Manes Funeral Home. People came from far and wide to his funeral. He had friends from Alabama, Georgia, Virginia, West Virginia, North Carolina, and Kentucky because of his faith in the Lord Jesus Christ and the signs of the gospel. Many of them came to the funeral on Tuesday, July 16, 1991.

In the afternoon I was appointed by John Brown to turn the media away from the funeral home. Bud (Marvin) Gregg preached his funeral. Marvin preached from John 3, "Ye must be born again."

After the service, the body was buried near his father in a cemetery where there are only a few graves. The private road to the cemetery also leads to the Holiness Church of God in Jesus' Name. The cemetery overflowed with people. Some lined the hillside; some set on the ground. We sang several old time gospel songs. Among them was "Amazing Grace." John Brown said that Jimmy Ray Williams was dedicated to his family and to his church and a hard worker and was a practitioner of the Word of God.

After Jimmy Ray was bitten, the media got news of what happened. Reporters from as far away as Los Angeles, New York, and Miami showed up. A film crew from CNN also showed up. The family of Jimmy Ray asked me to keep the reporters away from the funeral. They did not want any pictures taken. Just before the funeral began, a half-dozen reporters showed up. Fred Brown was among them. I asked them not to take pictures at the request of the family member. As I was talking one reporter said that if they didn't get the story somebody will print the story anyway. The *Examiner* got the story somehow and printed it.

Things just got out of hand. There was not much a man could do. We had to ask the funeral director to ask the reporters to leave the funeral home property. About an hour later, all the reporters were off the property. However, photographers with zoom lenses had stationed themselves across the railroad tracks at the corner of the old Valentine-Shults building. One photographer was a filming from a window in the county executive's office on the second floor of the courthouse.

The newspaper reported on Jimmy Ray, Jr.'s, death. One article was headed "Rattlesnake Kills Man during Church Service." It said churchgoer Jimmy Ray Williams, Jr., tested his fearless faith in the deadly bite of a 3-foot black rattlesnake and lost within forty-five minutes. It said his Holy Ghost minister, charismatic Pastor Marvin Bud Gregg of the snake-handling, strychnine-drinking House of Prayer in Jesus' Name church outside Morristown, Tennessee, assured twenty mourners that if they ever see Jimmy Ray again, they will see a crown of righteousness on his head. It said the unrepentant pastor told a Hamblen County sheriff's investigator on behalf of the thirty tight-lipped parishioners that Jimmy Ray was a good boy. He was quoted as saying that the Bible says if a man lays down his life for the gospel, he'll make it through the heavenly gates. It claimed that Williams's father had fatally challenged his own religious faith eighteen years earlier by drinking strychnine. It also noted that his stepfather Pastor Liston Pack, had been charged with a misdemeanor for handling snakes. It stated the he appealed the state law to the US Supreme Court, but it was not heard.

I think it was thrown out of court because Jimmy Carter was running for president at the time and this was a religious issue and it might hurt Jimmy Carter's chances to be elected president. Liston Pack told me that Jimmy Carter was a Baptist.

The newspaper reported that Hamblen County detective Larry Samsel told the examiner that serpent handling is pretty shocking stuff to most of us. However reportedly he said it's hard to put a case together without witnesses unless an officer was present during the service in which the snakebite occurred. The paper noted that Allen Williams dismissed his brother's death as an incident between and him and the Lord.

The newspaper reported that when asked whether his church intends to continue the practice, Pastor Gregg said, "I plan on preaching the gospel. Anything else I cannot comment on. White Pine Police Chief Jeff Manes was quoted as saying it would be difficult to bring charges in the case.

After the death of Jimmy Ray Williams, I was deeply trouble in my spirit. As I was asleep I had a night vision. I dreamed that I went to this place. It was a huge stone mountain. There was no way in or out but a round hole that is in the side of the stone. As I got to the huge Stone Mountain, I saw the prophets of old. Abraham appeared unto me. His hair was white. He had a white beard and wore a wool garment that reached down to his feet. He had a rod in his hand. Abraham told me I had to go into the huge stone and save someone out of it. He told me that when I went into the huge stone, it would catch on fire.

As I went in the huge stone, it began to burn. Inside the huge stone were many different passages. I heard someone hollering to save him from this fire. I heard another voice. It was a woman's voice. The flames and smoke were getting worse. I finally came to the room where the man was. I looked in and went closer. It was Jimmy Ray. I reached out and got him. I laid him on my shoulder and carried him through the flames. I could still hear the voice of the woman. It was a voice I recognized. I got outside the huge stone. By that time the stone was engulfed in flames. It burned to ashes before the fire went out. Then I heard a voice that said that Jimmy Ray was saved. Then I understood why the Lord took Jimmy Ray on home to be with Him. It was because of all the trouble that he was going through. Romans 8:28 says, "And we know that all things work together for good to them that love God. To them who are the called according to *his* purpose." Jimmy Ray's faith in God was strong and he endured to the end. The Bible says, "for we know that if our earthly house of this tabernacle were dissolved we have a building of God, house not made with hands, eternal in heavens" (1 Corinthians 5).

# Chapter 15

"And if any man shall take away from the words of the book of this prophecy, God shall take away his part out of the book of life, and out of the holy city, and from the things which are written in this book." (Revelation 22:19)

## The Death of Punkin Brown and the Battle for Custody of His Children

We finished building the Edwina Church of God in Jesus' Name in 1993. Two years later John Brown opened the Marshal Church. That same year, 1995, a Parrottville woman died from snakebite she received during a church service at Middlesboro, Kentucky. She was bit at Jammie Coots church, the Gospel Tabernacle in Jesus' Name. She was bit on Sunday, August 6, the last day of the homecoming. The lady was Melinda Francine Duvall Brown, the wife of one of John Brown's sons, Punkin Brown. She died of complications from the snakebite. She was twenty-eight.

Melinda was up front when she took a 4-foot black rattlesnake from her husband, John Punkin Brown, Jr. Ralph Hood was nearby when the serpent bit her on the left arm. Carl Porter of the Kingston, Georgia, church got the snake and put it back in the box. Two had handled the serpent or three other church members with victory before it struck Melinda.

Melinda set outside the church for a while trying to recover from the bite. She then was driven to Pastor Jamie Coot's home. He kept the ailing woman at his Middlesboro home where she suffered until an ambulance was called Tuesday at 3:38 P.M. For two days Melinda Brown refused medical treatment. She said she was trusting in the Lord.

However, she died from the bite. Her children were allowed to view her body at the Manes Funeral Home in Newport, Tennessee.

Melinda's husband and her five children were in church when she was bitten. The children were taken back home to Tennessee soon after the incident. Cocke County Juvenile Referee Phil Owens was quoted in the local paper, the *Observer*, as saying Melinda's parents, Francis Holden and Lewis Duvall Ashe of Cleveland, Tennessee, came to his office and expressed concern for the chilildren's safety. They told Owens that they believed poisonous snakes are kept at the Brown home. Ownes signed an order placing Brown's five children in the custody of a relative in Cleveland. The children ranged in age from eleven months to nine years at the time of Melinda's death.

Punkin Brown reportedly complained tearfully that his children were taken from his home in Parrottsville without his knowledge. He said he was handling arrangements for his wife's funeral when social workers from the Tennessee Department of Human Services and the sheriff's department came to his home and took his kids. He was quoted as saying that "The department of human service came in and took my kids out one at a time and asked them if they wanted to stay with me or their grandmother. They said they wanted to stay with me." Punkin said went to see a lawyer but he was unsympathetic to Punkin's plight.

The court ordered that the children be taken and placed in the custody of the Ashes. The Ashes filed a petition with the court for permanent custody of the children. Lewis said he and his wife believe the children would be better off living with them.

Later the paper reported that juvenile referee C. Philip Owens restored full custody of his five children to John Punkin Brown, Jr. The children had been in the temporary care of Brown's sister in law, Angelia Ashe, and her husband, William of Cleveland, Tennessee. William Ashe was quoted as saying he and other family would seek first-degree murder charges against Punkin Brown, Jr. They indicated they would seek charges against Pastor Jamie Coots.

In an August 14, 1995, letter, Bowling told Bell County. Kentucky attorney John Golden that he would not grant Golden's request to issue a criminal summons against either Brown or Coots. According to Kentucky law, Pastor Coots could be charged with a class C misdemeanor for allowing snake handling during his church's homecoming. However, Bowling wrote that his decision was based on the religious nature of the incident and the adverse media exposure it would bring the Eastern Kentucky region. He said that if the court were to permit this matter to come to trail, "I foresee a defendant Coots martyred by his church members while a gleeful media works overtime to enforce another label against Eastern Kentucky and Appalachia." Steven T. MacFarland, director of the Christian Legal Societies Center for Law and Religious freedom in Annandale, Virginia, stated that Kentucky's anti-serpent-handling law might not pass constitutional muster.

The first time I saw John Brown, Sr., was in Marshall, North Carolina, in 1976. It was at the House of Prayer in Jesus Christ's Name. Gene Raines was holding a meeting at the church. The second time was in the fall of 1977. John Brown, Sr., and John Fish were praying for Lester Raines. He had sugar. They stopped by my house and asked if I had any serpents. I said I had three big copperheads. One was jet black. John Brown, Sr., asked me to come to the Holiness Church of God in Jesus' Name in Carson Springs and bring the serpents that following week. That is the first time that I attended the Carson Springs church.

The service went good that night. It was the first time I saw John Punkin Brown, Jr. He was ten years old at the time. This was in 1977. The first time that Punkin Brown was serpent bit was in North Carolina. Punkin and Jimmy Ray, Jr., caught a big old mountain copperhead. It was red in color. They caught the snake in Carson Springs down below the church. The following week it was taken to the church in Marshall. During the service,

Punkin went to the serpent box and opened it. When he reached in a serpent bit him on the hand. John Brown, Sr., got the serpent. It tried to eat him up. It was striking and jumping at John, Sr. Finally, he got the copperhead back in the box. It was weeks before Punkin recovered from the serpent bite.

In 1980 we were in a church in Kingston, Georgia, the Church of the Lord Jesus' Christ. This is where John, Jr., met Melinda Duvall. They dated a while and later on got married at the House Prayer in Jesus' Christ Name in Marshall, North Carolina. They moved to Georgia. Melinda got with child. They name him Jonathan. Soon Punkin and Melinda moved back to Parrottsville, Tennessee. Punkin built a house down below his father and mother. Punkin got disabled with a bad back. Melinda took Jonathan with her and moved back to Georgia. After several months separation, Punkin started going down to Georgia and dating Melinda again. They got back together. Melinda had four more children, twins Jacob and Jeremiah, Sarah, and Daniel. Punkin Brown was widely known as a snake-handling evangelist. He preached from church to church and from state to state.

Melinda was buried in Carson Springs at the Holiness Church of God in Jesus' Name after her dying from the lethal bite she received at the Middlesboro homecoming. Eventually, juvenile referee C. Philip Owens restored full custody to Punkin Brown of his five children. Punkin lived with his five children in a trailer on Good Hope in Parrotisville, Tennessee.

The last three years of Punkin's life were largely spent in evangelizing. He preached from Jolo, West Virginia, to Sand Mountain, Alabama. While evangelizing at the Church of Lord Jesus in Jolo, West Virginia, he was bit by a rattlesnake. While he suffered he did not die. He was bit again at the House of Prayer in Jesus' Name in Harlan, Kentucky. He was preaching at Brother Burce Helton's church. After the service, he was trying to put up a rattlesnake when it bit him on the leg. His father John Brown, Sr., and mother, Peggy, and brother Mark and I went to Brother Helton's house to see Punkin. He was lying on the bed in pain while we prayed for him. Other church members sang. We stayed that night. Punkin was feeling better and in the morning, so I left for my home in Tennessee with brother Jimmy Ray Williams and sister Tersea. On the way back, we stopped on the mountain and got a drink of water that was coming out of the rocks. When we got to Newport, Jimmy Ray let me out. I got in my car that I had left at his home and drove the short distance to my house in Del Rio. Later that week, I went to Brother Punkin's house over in Parrottsville. He now lived in a white house off the bank. I stayed a good while, talking about the good old days with Punkin.

Once, Punkin, Allen Williams, and I went to Dry Fork to snake hunt. Allen had some little baby rattlesnakes in a box. Punkin had a pillowcase full of copperheads in it. As we were walking up the rocky Dry Fork road, he reached in and brought a handful out. One bit him on the hand. He seemed okay, so we came on out of the hollow and went home. That night Punkin went to the church in Morristown. He broke out in hives all over. It took a month to get over the bite.

In May of 1998, Punkin was hunting in North Carolina for rattlesnakes. It was hot and dry that year and snakes were hard to find. Punkin walked to the top of a rock cleft and saw a huge yellow rattlesnake between two flat rocks. He took his hook and pulled the snake out and put it in a pillowcase to carry it back off the mountain. He got in his car and headed back to Tennessee. This was the rattlesnake that would prove fatal to Punkin. It was this snake that bit him October 3, 1998, while he was preaching a revival at Billy Summerford's church on Sand Mountain.

A newspaper article was headed "Snake Handling Preacher Dies from Bite during a Church Service at the Rock Holiness Church on Sand Mountain." It reported that Punkin died within an hour of being bitten by the huge yellow timber rattlesnake he so often used to demonstrate his religious faith. It said Punkin died as he lived, in the faith. It said Punkin collapsed on the floor of the church just minutes after the 4-foot long yellow timber rattlesnake bit him on the finger. Church members said he had been handling the snake for about five minutes before he was

bitten. They said he put the snake back in the box, and within
three to four minutes, he went down on the church floor. He
reportedly refused to seek medical attention. Punkin was
pronounced dead at Jackson County Hospital in Scottsboro,
Alabama, about 10 miles from the Rock House Holiness Church.

Reverend Billy Summerford was quoted as saying his church
is the only church in the community that practices snake
handling. Punkin had reportedly been bitten twenty-two times
since he first started handling snakes at age seventeen. The
newspaper noted that Punkin had grown up in the serpent-
handling tradition. It was said he was strong in his faith and
continued to handle poisonous snakes even after the death of his
wife, Melinda, in 1995 from a rattlesnake bite.

Ralph Hood and I were at Punkin Brown's funeral. Before
leaving the funeral home in Newport, John Brown, Sr., led his
grandchildren to his son's silver casket for them to say goodbye to
their father. After patting his son's arm, Brown, Sr., turned
slowly and walked to his wife's side. Peggy Brown spent the final
minutes with her oldest son, leaning over the casket in mourning.
She tenderly cupped his face in her hands and kissed his forehead.

Many of these who filled the funeral home's chapel to
overflowing filed past the casket. Many touched Punkin's body,
wept, and walked on. Outside there was a steady drizzle of rain
falling. Punkin's casket was taken to a small church cemetery in a
deep hollow in Carson Springs. It is on a ridgeline at the top of
steep hill above the fomer Holiness Church of God in Jesus'
Name.

At the cemetery, several members pulled out rattlesnakes
from boxes they had brought to the cemetery. They began
handling the snakes while others were singing and praying. Some
cradled serpents in their fingers while others rubbed their heads
with open palms. I was handling a big black rattlesnake. Lydia
Elkins Hollins of the Jolo church in West Virginia took the
serpent from me. She cuddled the large black timber rattlesnake
in her arms like a baby. She then broke into dancing while
speaking in tongues. Punkin's brother, Mark, handled a

rattlesnake, as did Punkin's father, John, Sr., Billy Summerford, Jamie Coots, and other ministers gathered at the graveside and echoed the church's belief that Punkin Brown died because it was his appointed time to die. I believe we all are predestined before the foundation this world. Punkin was buried beside his wife, Melinda Brown. Over a hundred people were at the burial site.

After Punkin Brown's death, a custody battle was waged for the five Brown children who had now lost both parents to serpent bites. John and Peggy Brown, Sr., wished to have custody of the children. However, Melinda's family sought custody. The battle was waged in the Cocke County juvenile court. The court expressed concern that John Brown, Sr., was a serpent-handling minister with his own church in Marshall, North Carolina. Ralph Hood testified for the Brown family and told the court that being raised within the tradition did not endanger children. He noted that children are not allowed to handle serpents and are protected in services while serpents are being handled by the faithful. The local Newport newspaper ran an article headed "Snake Handlers' Orphans Divide Time between Dueling Relatives." It reported that after a court battle temporary custody for the Brown's children would be split between the two sets of grandparents. Noting that both the paternal and maternal grandparents were equally qualified, Judge Bell ruled that the minor children would stay with their maternal grandparents during the school years and with their paternal grandparents in the summer months and during holiday breaks.

# Chapter 16

"Ye serpents, ye generation of vipers how can ye escape the damnation of hell?" (Matthew 22:33)

## God Grants Me a Vision of Hell and the Power to Preach the Word

The sermon that Jesus Christ gave me on hell—What happens after death? Ecclesiastes 9:5: "For the living know that they shall die, but the dead know not anything neither have they any more a reward for the memory of them is forgotten. Does death befall both men and beasts." Ecclesiastes 3:19: "For that which befalleth the sons of men, befalleth beasts even one thing befalleth them: as the one dieth, so dieth the other; yea, they all have one breath, so that a man hath no preeminence above a beast, for all is vanity." Does the flesh, turn to dust again? Ecclesiastes 3:20: "All go unto one place: all are of the dust, and all turn to dust again." Genesis 3:19: "In the sweat of they face shalt thou eat bread, till thou return unto the ground, for out of it was thou taken, for dust thou art and unto dust shalt thou return." What place does Jesus say man goes to when he dies? Ecclessiastes 9:10: "Whatsoever they hath findeth to do, do it with thy might for there is no work nor device nor knowledge nor wisdom in the grave whither thou goes. Did Job realize he would go to the grave after death?" Job 17:13: "If I wait, the grave is mine house; I have made my bed in the darkness; was Jesus Christ made flesh?" John 1:14 "And the Word was made flesh and dwelt among us and we beheld His glory, the glory as the only begotten of the Father, full of grace and truth, did Christ take up on the same mortal flesh of which we are composed." Hebrews 2:14: "Forasmuch them as the children are partakers of flesh and blood, He also Himself likewise took part of the same that through death He might destroy him, that had the power of death, that is, the devil." Did Jesus Christ have to go to the grave as other mortal men do? Acts 2:31: "He seeing this before spake of the resurrection of Christ, that His soul was not left in hell, neither His flesh did see corruption, resurrected to judgment, when will the dead be judged." John 5:28–29: "Marvel not at this for the hour is coming in which all that are in the graves shall hear His voice, and shall come forth, they that have done good unto the resurrection of life, and they that have done evil unto the resurrection of damnation. Those who proved themselves to be wicked reserved for a future time of formal sentencing and punishment." 2 Peter 2:9: "The Lord knoweth how to deliver the godly out of temptation and to reserve the unjust unto the day of judgment to be punished." Revelation 20:13: "And the sea gave up the dead which were in it; and death and hell delivered up the dead which were in them; and they were judged every man according to their works." Death by fire? What is the wages of sin? Romans 6:23 "For the wages of sin is death, but the gift of God is eternal life through Jesus Christ, our Lord." What does Paul warn will be the judgment of those who willfully sin against God? Hebrews 10:26–27: "For if we sin wilfully after that we have received the knowledge of the truth, there remaineth no more sacrifice for sins but a certain fearful looking for of judgment and fiery indignation which shall devour the adversaries."

Does Jesus Christ compare false ministers who don't bring forth good works to trees that will be burned up? Matthew 7:15–19: "Beware of false prophets which come to you in sheep's clothing but inwardly they are ravening wolves; ye shall know them by their fruits. Do men gather grapes of thorns or figs of thistles, even so every good tree bringeth forth good fruit, but a corrupt tree bringeth forth evil fruit; a good tree cannot bring forth evil fruit neither can a corrupt tree bring forth good fruit;

every tree that bringeth not forth good fruit is hewn down and
cast into fire."

What did Jesus Christ say to unrepentent scribes and
pharisees of His day? Matthew 23:33: "Ye serpents, ye
generation of vipers how can ye escape the damnation of hell?"

What did Christ warn would happen to those who will not
repent of their sinful ways? Luke 13:3–5: "I tell you, nay, except
ye repent, ye shall likewise perish."

Did Jesus Christ show by His parable of the tares that there
is to be a future harvest? Matthew 13:24–30: "Another parable
put He forth unto them, saying the King of heaven is likened
unto a man which sowed good seed in his field, but while men
slept, his enemy came and sowed tares among the wheat, and
went his way, but when the blade was sprung up, and brought
forth fruit, then appeared the tares also, so the servant of the
householder came and said unto him, sir, didst not thou sow good
seed in they field, from whence then hath it tares, he said unto
them, an enemy hath done this. The servants said unto him, wilt
thou then that we go and gather them up, but he said nay, let
them grow together until the harvest, and in the time of harvest
I will say to the reapers, gather ye together first the tares and
bind them in bundles to burn them, but gather the wheat into
my barn."

Does Psalm 37:20 also show the fate of the wicked will be
tormented by fire? "But the wicked shall perish and the enemies
of the Lord shall be as the fat of lambs they shall consume into
smoke shall they consume away."

Is there coming a time that will be flaming hot? So hot that
it will torment and consume the wicked? Malachi 4:1: "For
behold the day cometh that shall burn as an oven, and all the
proud, yea, and all that do wickedly, shall stubble and the day that
cometh shall burn them up saith the Lord of Hosts that it shall
leave them neither root nor branch."

Will Satan and his demons burn the wicked up, or the
Eternal Jesus Christ Malachi 4:3: "And ye shall tread down the

wicked for they shall be ashes under the soles of your feet, in the day that I shall do this, saith the Lord of Hosts."

What is the Lake of Fire? Are all who refuse to repent finding themselves in a lake of fire and brimstone? Revelation 21:8: "But the fearful and unbelieving and the abominable and murders and idolators, and all liars shall have their part in the lake which burneth with fire and brimstone which is the second death."

Does Revelation 20:13–15 prove the fact the wicked will be cast in the Lake of Fire after judgment? "And the sea gave up the dead which were in it; and death and hell delievered up the dead which were in them; and they were judged every man according to their works and death and hell were cast into the lake of fire, this is the second death."

Will all mortals whose name is not written in the Book of Life be cast into the Lake of Fire? Revelation 20:15: "And whosoever was not found written in the Book of Life was cast in the Lake of Fire."

When does the Lake of Fire begin at Christ's second coming? Revelation 19:20: "And the beast was taken with him the false prophet that wrought miracles before him with which he and them that worshipped his image, these both were cast alive into a lake of fire burning with brimstone."

Is this fire everlasting? Matthew 25:4: "Then shall He say also unto them on the left hand, depart from Me, ye cursed, into everlasting fire, prepared for the devil and his angels."

Much later, after the Thousand Years Reign will the flames of the Lake of Fire purify the earth's surface? 2 Peter 3:10: "But the day of the Lord will come as a thief in the night in which the heavens shall pass away with a great noise and the elements shall melt with fervent heat, the earth also and the works that are therein shall be burned up."

Will Satan be cast in to the Lake of Fire? Revelation 20:10: "And the devil that deceived them was cast into the lake of fire and brimstone where the beast and the false prophet are, and shall be, tormented day and night for ever and ever."

Did John the Baptist ever speak of unquenchable fire?
Matthew 3:12: "Whose fan is in his hand he will thoroughly
purge his floor and gather his wheat into the garner but he will
burn up the chaff with unquenchable fire." This same verse is
also recorded in Luke 3:17.

Did Jesus Christ say that hell fire will never be quenched?
Mark 9:43–48: "And if thy hand offend thee, cut it off, it is
better for thee to enter into life maimed than having two hands
to go into hell, in the fire that never shall be quenched, and if
thy foot offend thee, cut it off, it is better for thee to enter half
into life than having two feet to be cast into hell, into the fire
that never shall be quenched, where their worm dieth not and the
fire is not quenched. And if thine eye offend thee, pluck it out, it
is better for thee to enter into the Kingdom of God with one eye
than having two eyes to be cast into hell fire where their worm
dieth not and the fire is not quenched."

Lazarus and the Rich Man as told in Luke 16:19–31: "There
was a certain rich man which was clothed in purple and fine
linen, and fared sumptuously ever day; and there was a certain
beggar named Lazarus which was laid at his gate, full of sores, and
desiring to be fed with the crumbs which fell from the rich
man's table. Moreover the dogs came and licked his sore and it
come to pass, that the beggar died and was carried by the angels
into Abraham's bosom. The rich man also died and was buried,
and in hell he lifted up his eyes being in torment, and seeth
Abraham afar off, and Lazarus in his bosom. And he cried, and
said, 'Father Abraham have mercy on me, and send Lazarus that
he may dip the tip of his finger in water and cool my tongue for I
am tormented in this lame.' But Abraham said, 'Son, remember
that thou in thy lifetime received thy good things but likewise
Lazarus evil things, but now he is comforted and thou art
tormented, and beside all this between us and you there is a great
gulf fixed so that they which would pass from hence to you
cannot neither can they pass to us that would come from hence.'
Then he said, 'I pray thee therefore, Father, that Thou wouldest
send him to my father's house for I have brethen that he may

testify unto them lest they also come into this place of torment.'
Abraham saith unto him, 'They have Moses and the prophets, let
them hear them.' And he said, 'Nay, Father Abraham, but if one
went unto them from the dead, they will repent, ' and he said
unto him, 'If they hear not Moses and the prophets neither will
they be persuaded through one risen from the dead.'"

At the last judgment, at the resurrection of the wicked, both
the dead and he rich man is going to be cast into the Lake of Fire,
and the Lord said that whosoever was not found written in the
Book of Life was cast into the Lake of Fire, this is the second
death. There is no future resurrection out of the Lake of Fire, it
is forever and ever, there is not getting out, it is eternal hell fire.
The Bible say in Revelation 14:11: "And the smoke of their
torment ascendeth up for ever and ever: and they have no rest day
nor night, who worship the beast and his image, and whosoever
receiveth the mark of his name."

## The True Gospel with the Signs Following

Nearly 2, 000 years ago, Jesus came to this earth to preach the
words of the Father. John 12:49: "For I have not spoken of
Myself; the Father which sent Me, he gave me a commandment,
what I should say and what I should speak." John 14:24: "He that
loveth Me not keepeth not My saying and the word which ye
hear is not Mine, but the Father's which sent Me." John 14:10:
"Believest thou not that I am in the Father, and the Father in
Me? The words that I speak unto you I speak not of Myself, but
the Father that dwelleth in Me, He doeth the works."

What message did Jesus Christ preach? Mark 1:14: "Now
after that John was put in prison Jesus came in to Galilee
preaching the gospel of the Kingdom God."

Did Jesus say one must believe the Gospel? Mark 1:15: "And
saying, the time is fulfilled and the Kingdom of God is at hand,
repent, and believe the gospel." Mark 16:15–20: "And He said

unto them, 'Go ye into all the world and preach the word to every creature. He that believeth and is baptized shall be saved, but he that believeth shall not be damned and these signs shall follow them that believeth in My name shall they cast out devils, they shall speak with new tongues, they shall take up serpents, if they drink any deadly thing it shall not hurt them; they shall lay hands on the sick and they shall recover.' So thenafter the Lord had spoken unto them He was received up into heaven and sat on the right hand of God and they went forth and preached everywhere, the Lord working with them and confirming the word with signs following. Amen."

Did Jesus Christ send forth His Apostles and true disciples to preach the same gospel with signs following? Luke 9:1–2: "Then He called His twelve disciples together and gave them power and authority over all devils and to cure diseases and He sent them to preach the Kingdom of God and to heal the sick."

Was His gospel of the Kingdom of God with signs following to be preached in all the world just before the end, and his Second Coming? Matthew 24:14: "And this gospel of the Kingdom shall be preached in all the world for a witness unto all nations, and then the end shall come." Mark 13:10: "And the gospel must first be published among all nations."

Did Phillip preach the same gospel? Acts 8:12: "But when they believed Phillip preaching the things concerning the Kingdom of God, and the Name of Jesus Christ, they were baptized, both men and women."

What did the apostle Paul preach? Acts 19:8: "And he went into the synagogue and spake boldly for the space of three months, disputing and persuading the things concerning the Kingdom of God." Acts 14:22: "Confirming the souls of the disciples and exhorting them to continue in the faith, and that we must through much tribulation enter into the Kingdom of God."

Did Paul preach the same gospel among the Gentiles at Ephesus? Acts 20:25: "And now, behold, I know that ye all among whom I have gone preaching the Kingdom of God shall see my face no more. Did Paul preach the same gospel to both Jews and

Gentiles in Rome?" Acts 28:23: "And when they had appointed him a day, there came many to him into his lodging, to whom he expounded and testified the Kingdom of God, persuading them concerning Jesus, both out of the law of Moses, and the prophet from morning to evening." Acts 28:31: "Preaching the Kingdom of God, and teaching those things concerning the Lord Jesus Christ with all confidence, no man forbidding him."

Did some false disciple, in Paul's day, try to pervert the gospel of Christ with the signs following? Galatians 1:6–7: "I marvel that ye are soon removed from Him that called you into the grace of Christ unto another gospel, which is not another, but there be some people that trouble you and would pervert the gospel of Christ." What judgment or decision is given on any who would try to preach any other gospel? Galatians 1:8: "but thought we, or an angel from heaven preach any other gospel unto you than that which we have preached unto you, let him be accursed." Was it really a twofold curse? Galatians 1:9: "As we said before, so I now say again, if any man preach any other gospel unto you than that ye have received, let him be accursed." The Bible shows there is only one true gospel, the gospel that Jesus Christ preached.

The gospel of the Kingdom of God with signs following to understand the first sign. "In My Name shall they cast out devils." The Greek word devils means demons. Was a demon always a demon before they became demons? Let us study the scriptures to see what a demon was before it became a demon. Did God create all things by Jesus Christ? Ephesians 3:9: "And to make all men see what is the fellowship of the mystery which from the beginning of the world hath been hid in God, who created all things by Jesus Christ." Colossians 1:16–18: "For by Him were all things created by Him and for Him and He is before all things and by Him all things consist and He is the head of the body, the church, who is the beginning, the first born from the dead, that in all things he might have preeminence."

How did Jesus Christ create the universe and everything that exists? Psalm 33:6–9: "By the Word of the Lord were the heavens made, and all the host of them by the breath of His Mouth. He gathereth the waters of the sea together as an heap; He layeth up the depth in store houses. Let all the earth fear the Lord, let all the inhabitants of the world stand in awe of Him, for He spake, and it was done, he commanded, and it stood fast." Psalm 104:30: "Thou sendest forth thy spirit, they are created, and Thou renewest the face of the earth." Genesis 1:2–3: "And the earth was without form and void, and darkness was upon the face of the deep and the spirit of God moved upon the face of the waters and God said, Let there be light and there was light." Jesus spoke and the Holy Spirit and His power responds and does what Jesus Christ commands.

Did Jesus Christ create the entire universe when earth was created? Genesis 1:1: "In the beginning God created the heavens and the earth."

What does the Bible reveal was created before the material creation? Job 38:4–7: "Where wast thou when I laid the foundations of the earth. Declare, if thou hast understanding, who hath laid the measures thereof, if thou knowest. Or who hath stretched the line upon it? Whereupon are the foundations thereof fastened? Or who laid the cornerstone thereof; and the morning stars sang together and all the sons of God shouted for joy?" (In verse 7, morning stars and sons of God refers to angels.)

What verse clearly shows that the earth was not in confusion and a wasteland when first created? Isaiah 45:18: "For thus saith the Lord that created the heavens; God himself that formed the earth and made it; He hath established it, He created it not in vain (or confusion) He formed it to be inhabited; I am the Lord and there is none else." We find in Job 38:4–7 that the angels God created were shouting for joy at the creation of earth. The Bible does not give details about how long the angels lived on earth, before the creation of man.

Did Jesus Christ also create his Laws and his goverment? Colossians 1:16: "For by Him were all things created, that are in heaven, and are in earth, visible and invisible, whether they be thrones, or dominions, or principalities or powers; all things were created by Him." Jesus Christ set His government with His constitution and laws, over His entire creations, and the great archangel, Lucifer, was placed on a throne to carry out Jesus Christ's government on earth. Jesus Christ's government and His laws, by which Lucifer was to rule the other angels, was a way of life. Agreement of feeling, ideas, or actions, getting along well together or work in perfect harmony, and in peace. Lucifer and one-third of the angels on earth did something for the earth to become wasted and empty and in confusion. Genesis 1:2: "And the earth was without form and void; and darkness was upon the face of the deep; and the spirit of God moved upon the face of the waters." Genesis 1:1 shows that heaven and the earth was created; verse 2 shows that the earth was without form and was in confusion. Let's look more in the Bible and see what caused that confusion on the earth. Did Lucifer continue to carry Jesus Christ's government on earth, according to His way of life, or did Lucifer rebel and, thereby, sin greatly? Was Lucifer one of the anointed cherubs (angels) who covered Christ's throne? Ezekiel 28:14: "Thou art the anointed cherubs who covereth and I set thee so thou was upon the holy mountain of God; thou hast walked up and down in the midst of the stones of fire."

Did Lucifer decide to leave the earth and ascend to heaven in an attempt to exalt his throne (which was in Eden) in the garden of God, above all the angels or the star of God? Ezekiel 28:13: "Thou hast been in Eden (notice the word "Eden") the garden of God; ever precious stone was thy covering, the sardius, topaz, and the diamond, the beryl, the onyx and the jasper, the sapphire, the emerald and the carbuncle, and the gold, the workmanship of thy tabrets and of they pipes was prepared in the day that wast created." Isaiah 14:14: "I will ascend above the heights of the clouds; I will be like the most High."

Lucifer had nothing less in his mind than knocking the Creator, Jesus Christ, off His throne and becoming the supreme ruler himself. Lucifer, the super archangel, was perfect in all ways from the day of his creation until something happened in him.

What was found in Lucifer? Ezekiel 28:15: "Thou was perfect in thy way from the day that thou wast created, til iniquity was found in thee."

Did he become vain and corrupt in his wisdom? Ezekiel 28:17: "Thine heart was lifted up because of thy beauty, thou hast corrupted thy wisdom by reason of they brightness, I will cast thee to the ground, I will lay thee before kings, that they may behold thee."

When Lucifer began thinking thoughts of hate feeling and showing hatefulness and had a bad desire and imagination. He began to think unreasonably and his mind turned from the right way or from the turth to his own way. He become totally demented a lunatic, mad, senseless, wild. Lucifer was no longer content with rule of the earth, he wanted to take over the universe. Lucifer made his angels feel discontent and wronged by Jesus Christ. Lucifer deceived them by turning their minds to disobedence amd away from the goverment of Jesus Christ.

What happened to Lucifer and his angels as a result of their attempt to take control of the universe from their Creator, Jesus Christ? Isaiah 14:12: "How art thou fallen from heaven, O Lucifer, son of the morning! how art thou cut down to the ground, which didst weaken the nations!" Revelation 12:3–4: "And there appeared another wonder in heaven; and behold a great red dragon, having seven heads and ten horns, and seven crowns upon his heads. And his tail drew the third part of the stars of heaven, and did cast them to the earth; and the dragon stood before the woman which was ready to be delivered, for to devour her child as soon as it was born."

How did Jesus Christ tell about Lucifer or Satan's fall from heaven? Luke 10:18: "And He said unto them, I behold Satan as lightning fall from heaven." Lucifer became his Maker's adversary. That was his choice, not Jesus Christ's. So Jesus Christ changed his name to Satan which means adversary, competitor, enemy. Also, the angels were cast back to earth with him and became known as demons.

Does the Bible show that Lucifer and one-third of the angels left their habitation? Jude 1:6: "And the angels which kept not their first estate, but left their habitation, he hath reserved in everlasting chains under darkness unto the judgment of the great day." Michael, the great prince, and two-thirds of the angels remained loyal to Jesus Christ. They did not leave their habitation, which was heaven, to carry out the government of Jesus Christ. The Bible shows that when Lucifer and one-third of the angels left earth to take over the throne of Jesus Christ, Michael and the remaining angels were loyal. In Revelation 12:7: "There was a war in heaven and Michael and his angels fought against the dragon (or Satan). The dragon fought and one of his angels; they did not prevail and their place in heaven was lost and the great dragon was cast out to earth and his angels were cast out with him."

Does the Bible plainly state that Lucifer and his angels sinned? 2 Peter 2:4: "For if God spared not the angels that sinned, but cast them down to hell, and delivered them into chains of darkness, to be reserved unto judgment." We see that the Bible shows the earth was not created in confusion. Jesus Christ is not the author of confusion but Satan is because he and his angels sinned. That's what caused confusion on earth. The next step in the plan of Jesus Christ was to renew the face of the earth. Psalm 104:30: "Thou sendest forth thy spirit, they are created: and thou renewest the face of the earth." In Genesis 1:3 and the rest of the chapter, Jesus Christ is renewing the face of the earth. During the six work days—the first day He created light and darkness, or day and night; the second day He made the firmament of heaven; the third day He made the earth, seas, and grass; the fourth day He made the sun, moon, and stars; the fifth day He made the fowl, whales, and everything which the water brought forth; and on the sixth day He made the living creatures—cattle, beasts of the earth, and creeping things. God said, Let us make man in our image.

Did Jesus Christ give Adam and Eve some important knowledge? Genesis 2:16–17: "And the Lord God commanded the

man, saying, 'Of every tree of the garden thou mayest freely eat;
But of the tree of the knowledge of good and evil, thou shalt not
eat of it: for in the day that thou eatest thereof thou shalt surely
die.'"

Did Satan deceive Eve into disbelieving God and disobeying
His command? Genesis 3:1–7: "Now the serpent was more subtil
than any beast of the field which the Lord God had made. And he
said unto the woman, 'Yeah, hath God said, Ye shall not eat of
every tree of the garden?' And the woman said unto the serpent,
'We may eat of the fruit of the trees of the garden: But of the
fruit of the tree which is in the midst of the garden, God hath
said, Ye shall not eat of it, neither shall ye touch it, lest ye die.'
And the serpent said unto the woman, 'Ye shall not surely die:
For God doth know that in the day ye eat thereof, then your eyes
shall be opened, and ye shall be as gods, knowing good and evil.'
And when the woman saw that the tree was good for food, and
that it was pleasant to the eyes, and a tree to be desired to make
one wise, she took of the fruit thereof, and did eat it, and gave
also unto her husband with her, and he did eat. And the eyes of
them both were opened, and they knew that they were naked; and
they sewed fig leaves together, and made themselves aprons."

What happened to Adam's and Eve's minds after they chose
the way of Satan? The devil's attitude of discontent entered into
their minds. Satan was the first to sin and he caused one-third of
the angels to disobey, against God and sin, then he caused Eve to
sin and Adam to take of the forbidden fruit and sin. Does the
Bible show clearly that the world wide sin brings worldwide
destruction? 2 Peter 2:5: "And spared not the old world, but saved
Noah, the eighth person, a preacher of righteousness, bringing in
the flood upon the world of the ungodly." Genesis 6:5–13: "And
God saw that the wickedness of man was great in the earth, and
that every imagination of the thoughts of his heart was only evil
continually. And it repented the Lord that He had made man on
the earth, and it grieved Him at His heart. And the Lord said, 'I
will destroy man whom I have created from the face of the earth;
both man, and beast, and the creeping thing, and the fowls of the

air; for it repenteth Me that I have made them. But Noah found grace in the eyes of the Lord. These are the generations of Noah; Noah was a just man and perfect in his generations, and Noah walked with God. And Noah begat three sons, Shem, Ham and Japheth. The earth also was corrupt before God, and the earth was filled with violence. And God looked upon the earth, and, behold, it was corrupt, for all flesh had corrupted His way upon the earth. And God said unto Noah, 'The end of all flesh is come before Me, for the earth is filled with violence through them; and, behold, I will destroy them with the earth.'" This passage shows that worldwide human sin brought world destruction to the earth's surface; all men worldwide had sinned—only Noah walked with God. So the flood destroyed all human life on earth except Noah and his family.

After the flood the fallen angels, or demons, entered man at Sodom and Gomorrah and they became homosexuals. 2 Peter 2:6: "And turning the cities of Sodom and Gomorrha into ashes condemned them with an overthrow, making them an example unto those that after should live ungodly." Romans 1:26–27: "For this cause God gave them up unto vile affections: for even their women did change the natural use into that which is against nature: And likewise also the men, leaving the natural use of the woman, burned in their lust one toward another; men with men working that which is unseemly, and receiving in themselves that recompence of their error which was meet." Genesis 19:4–13: "But before they lay down, the men of the city, even the men of Sodom, compassed the house round, both old and young, all the people from every quarter. And they called unto Lot, and said unto him, 'Where are the men which came in to thee this night? bring them out unto us, that we may know them.' And Lot went out at the door unto them, and shut the door after him, And said, 'I pray you, brethren, do not so wickedly. Behold now, I have two daughters which have not known men; let me, I pray you, bring them unto you, and do ye to them as is good in your eyes: only unto these men do nothing; for therefore came they under the shadow of my roof.' And they said, 'Stand back.' And they said

again, 'This one fellow came in to sojourn, and he will needs be a
judge; now will we deal worse with thee, than with them.' And
they pressed sore upon the man, even Lot, and came near to
break the door. But the men put forth their hand, and pulled Lot
into the house to them, and shut to the door. And they smote the
men that were at the door of the house with blindness, both
small and great: so that they wearied themselves to find the door.
And the men said unto Lot, 'Hast thou here any besides? son in
law; and and thy sons, and thy daughters, and whatsoever thou hast
in the city, bring them out of this place; For we will destroy this
place, because the cry of them is waxen great before the face of
the Lord; and the Lord hath sent us to destroy it.' And Lot went
out, and spake unto his sons in law, which married his daughters,
and said, 'Up, get you out of this place; for the Lord will destroy
this city.' But he seemed as one that mocked unto his sons in
law." The Bible says that then the Lord rained upon Sodom and
upon Gomorrah brimstone and fire. The homosexuality and other
sins of Sodom and Gomorrah spread over the entire territory of
those cities and fiery, physical destruction came from God to the
entire area. The sins of the angels, which occurred before man
was created, was worldwide which caused the physical destruction
of the entire race of the earth.

The homosexuals were not born that way—a demon has
entered in them. The angels that were created cannot reproduce
and knew that they cannot, so Lucifer and his fallen angels enter
into the human race and both men and women become
homosexuals whom cannot reproduce. Satan knows the human
race will be destroyed. Today, homosexuals are being destroyed by
AIDS. They die and leave no children. The homosexuals can be
set free from the demons that have overtaken their minds. If
they would go to church, a church that believes in the five signs
with a true preacher of God would cast out their demons in the
name of Jesus Christ, they would be saved.

The demons, or fallen angels, recognized who Jesus Christ
was. Matthew 8:29: "And, behold, they cried out, saying, what
have we to do with thee, Jesus, thou Son of God? Art thou come

hither to torment us before the time? Are there demons that make people blind and dumb?" Matthew 12:22: "Then was brought unto Him one possessed with a devil, blind, and dumb; and He healed him, insomuch that the blind and dumb both spake and saw."

Did Jesus Christ give power to the disciples to cast out demons? Matthew 10:1: "And when He had called unto Him His twelve disciples, He gave them power against unclean spirits, to cast them out, and to heal all manner or disease." Mark 16:17: "And these signs shall follow them that believe; in My name shall they cast out devils; they shall speak with new tongues."

Did Jesus Christ cast out demons? Luke 4:41: "And devils also came out of many, crying out, and saying, Thou art Christ the Son of God. And He rebuking them suffered them not to speak; for they knew that He was Christ."

Did Jesus Christ give the seventy power to cast out demons? Luke 10:17: "And the seventy returned again with joy, saying, Lord, even the devils are subject unto us through Thy Name."

Did Jesus Christ give Peter power to cast out demons? Luke 5:16: "There came also a multitude out of the cities round about unto Jerusalem, bringing sick folks, and them which were vexed with unclean spirits; and they were healed every one. Did Jesus Christ give Paul the power to cast out demons?" Acts 16:16: "And it came to pass, as we went to prayer, a certain damsel possessed with a spirit of divination met us, which brought her masters much gain by soothsaying." Acts 17: "The same followed Paul and us, and cried, saying, These men are the servants of the most high God, which shew unto us the way of salvation." Verse 18: "And this did she many days. But Paul, being grieved, turned and said to the spirit, 'I command thee in the name of Jesus Christ to come out of her.' And he came out the same hour." Did Jesus Christ give Phillip the power to cast out demons?" Acts 8:7: "For unclean spirits, crying with loud voice, came out of man that were possessed with them: and many taken with palsies, and that were lame, were healed."

Today, the Church of the Living God is still casting out demons by the power of God and by the name of Jesus Christ. The true preachers of God believe in the five signs of God's word—people that are possessed can be set free if they go to a church that believes in the five signs. The first sign of casting out demons, the preacher will lay his hand upon their head and rebuke the demon in the name of Jesus Christ that the demons are cast out. Man can do nothing—Jesus Christ is the power, the attorney. The Bible says the devils also believe and tremble. This is the fist sign—they shall cast out devils.

The second sign—they shall speak in new tongues (in Greek translation—they shall speak in two tongues). Let us study more on the Day of the Pentecost. Acts 2:1–12: "And when the day of Pentecost was fully come, they were all with one accord in one place. And suddenly there came a sound from heaven as of a rushing mighty wind, and it filled all the house where they were sitting. And there appeared unto them cloven tongues, like as of fire, and it sat upon each of them. And they were all filled with the Holy Ghost, and began to speak with other tongues, as the Spirit gave them utterance. And there were dwelling at Jerusalem Jews, devout men, out of every nation under heaven. Now when this was noised abroad, the multitude came together, and were confounded, because that every man heard them speak in his own language. And they were all amazed and marvelled, saying one to another, 'Behold, are not all these which speak Galilaeans? And how hear we every man in our own tongue, wherein we were born Parthians, and Medes, and Elamites, and the dwellers in Mesopotamia, and in Judaea, and Cappadocia, in Pontus, and Aisa. Phyrgia, and Pamphylia, in Egypt, and in the parts of Libya about Cyrene, and strangers of Rome, Jews and proselytes. Cretes and Arabians, we do hear them speak in our tongues the wonderful works of God.' And they were all amazed, and were in doubt, saying one to another, 'What meaneth this?'" The sign of the new tongues in Mark is the same as that given on the day of Pentecost. The gift of tongues in 1 Corinthians 12:10: "To another the working of miracles; to another prophecy; to another discerning of spirits; to another divers kinds of tongues; to another the interpretation of tongues. 1 Corinthians 14: "If any man speaks in an unknown tongue, let it be by two, or, at the most, three and that by course and let one interpret, wherefore tongues are for a sign, wherefore let him that speaketh in an unknown tongue pray that he may interpret, but if there be no interpreter, let him keep silence in the church; and let him speak to himself, and to God. The man that speaks in tongues and there is an interpreter, then the revelation is known and it edifieth the church."

One time a woman was speaking in tongues at a church service and she was interpreting also. She said that the shield was down on the serpent handling and some were going to get bitten. That was in the month of April. It came to pass, as she interpreted, in July that same year, a man got bitten. The Bible says, "He that hath an ear, let him hear what the spirit saith unto the churhes."

The third sign—they shall take up serpents. Luke 10:19: "Behold, I give unto you power to tread on serpents and scorpions, and over all the power of the enemy: and nothing shall by any means hurt you. Serpent handling is a sign to confirm the Word. If a preacher is preaching the Word and feels the anointing to handle a serpent, Jesus Christ will give him victory over it. It takes the anointing of God to do the five signs

During the 1940s in Grasshopper Valley, Tennessee, at the Dolly Pond Church of God with the signs following, they kept a glass of strychnine on the pulpit—a tiny drop of which on a grain of corn would kill a chicken—and the anointed in the church would drink from this glass without any serious side effects. In another church in Kentucky, a man brought a glass of strychnine to one of their services. A man at this church got anointed, got the glass of strychnine and drank it in the Name of Jesus Christ and remained healthy and unharmed.

The fifth sign—they shall lay hands on the sick, and they shall recover. Diving healing did not end with the earthly ministry of Jesus. Rather, it has been carried forward by his followers, those who believe Jesus is still alive and still heals. Jesus said certain signs would follow those who believe in Him and among those are they that shall lay hands on the sick and the sick shall recover. James 5:14–15: "Is any sick among you? Let him call for the elders of the church; and let them pray over him, anointing him with oil in the name of the Lord: And the prayer of faith shall save the sick, and the Lord shall raise him up; and if he have committed sins, they shall be forgiven him."

If any man or woman tries to do any of the signs is in great danger of losing their lives. They have to be born again by the spirit of God—to handle serpents or to drink poison or to speak in tongues or cast out demons or to lay hands on the sick. The way to be born again is to repent of their sins. Acts 2:38: "Then Peter said unto them, 'Repent and be baptized every one of you in the name of Jesus Christ for the remission of sins, and ye shall receive the gift of the Holy Ghost.'"

# Chapter 17

"One generation passeth away, and another generation cometh; but the earth abidith forever" (Ecclesiastes 1:4)

## The Family Tree of James E. Morrow

This is the true story of the Naillons, my far off descendants. It was in the year of 1700. There was a very large track of land that was called the Cowee Nation. Indians lived there. They were Cherokees, members of a North American Indian tribe of the Iroquoians. This was before North Carolina became a state in 1789 and before Tennessee became the sixteenth state in 1796. At that time it was also called Naillon Town.

The Naillons and their family had to cross the Pigeon River to come in to what today is called Cocke County, Tennessee. They built a large family cabin out of logs on the bank of the river. They only had picks and mattocks and shovels and a cross cut saw to clear the land. They built the cabin facing the Tennessee and the Pigeon rivers. They used rocks and mud for the chimney and fireplace. They built a wagon road to the valley that is now called Hartford, Tennessee. They had a swinging foot log across the Pigeon River. The Naillons also built a ferryboat to carry logs and wagons and mules across to the other side of the Tennessee River.

The Naillons came form Ireland in the late 1600s. Patrick Naillon was born in 1769. He was my great-great-great-great grandpa. He was married to Frances Russell. She was born in 1790.

This story was told to me by Bertha L. Arrington my grandma. It was handed down to her from far off descendants. This is what was told.

One Francis Russell Naillon, my great-great-great-great grandma, went to the barn. What she saw filled her with great fear. She was frightened so much the hair raised up on her head and the back of her neck. There was the largest ratter snake that she ever saw and it was swallowing a baby lamb. It was a foot in diameter and 8 foot long. It had a head as big as a man's hands.

Francis Naillon went back to the house. About noon Patrick Naillon come in for dinner. Francis told Patrick about the giant ratter snake and Patrick got the muzzle-loader and went to the barn. What he saw made fear go through him. The rattlesnake was still lying and digestion the baby lamb. Patrick shot it dead.

His son, Elijah Washington Naillon, was just a boy. Patrick sent him to tell all the kinfolks, the Browna and the Moores and the Coggins to come to the Naillon barn. What the people saw that day was mind staggering. They hesitated and became confused. It will make your skin crawl to hear what they saw. The rattlesnake was skin out and the hide was put on the barn wall too dry. The women cooked the rattlesnake meat. They made rattlesnake stew. Forty people saw the giant dead rattlesnake. People still talk about it today.

While preaching a revival in Alabama nearly 200 years later my best friend, John Brown, Jr. (mostly called "Punkin"), was killed by a rattlesnake. The rattlesnake that killed him was caught in Naillon town at the same den that the giant rattlesnake come from that was killed by Patrick Naillon nearly 200 years ago. The den is above the tunnel in North Carolina, going up Interstate 40 to Heywood County.

William Moore was born in New Jersey in 1772. He was married to Nancy Cope. William Moore and Nancy Cope Moore were my great-great-great-great grandpa and grandma on the Moore side. This story was told to me by grandma. She told it to me while I was eating a Moon Pie and drinking an orange drink that we got out of the cold spring where we had put them in that morning. We had bought them at Timman Ball's store.

I listen to grandma Bertha Arrington as she told how her great-great-grandpa and grandma William Moore and Nancy Cope Moore told about a woman that put her baby in a cave. The woman lived up river. She had a daughter that had a child out of wedlock. She was dating a man who hated children. He told the woman that if she did not get rid of the baby he was going to quit dating her. One night while her mother was asleep the woman got up and got her baby and came down river. She crossed the river and put the baby in a cave, but the baby kept crawling out of the cave. The devil told the woman to take the baby back in the cave and lay a rock on its' dress so it could not crawl out. When the baby was found it was frozen to death. The rock was on the dress. The woman was put in jail for the rest of her life. This was in the 1800s.

Grandma Bertha also told me that their cabin was built on a large, flat rock and the fireplace was built on it. It was in the fall when William and Nancy moved into it. They had eighteen children. The winter was coming on. As the night got colder they built a fire. Early one morning the fire died down. One of the girls got up and saw a rattlesnake that was laying on the flat rock warning itself from the heat. The rattlesnake bit the girl. She was found dead the next morning.

Grandma Bertha also told me about the panther that ripped out the eye of the old family dog, Shuffle. Nancy Cope Moore sewed it back in with thread made from a mule hair. Shuffle had a white speck in that eye the rest of his life.

Grandma Bertha also told me about the eagle that carried a baby off. This was in the early 1800s. There were plenty of eagles then. An eagle was soaring in the sky. Suddenly it sweeps down along the great Pigeon River, catching fish, and flying back to the mountain on the other side where the rattlesnake den was. One day Nancy Cope Moore was washing clothes. Washing clothes for all the children was an everyday chore. While Nancy was washing on an old washboard she heard an eagle holler with a

high-pitched scream. Nancy looked up and saw a bald eagle
soaring on the wind across the deep blue sky. The eagle had a
baby and was flying to its nest on the other side the river. Nancy
hollered at Frances and told her that she is going to the eagle's
nest to get the baby. Nancy crossed the river. About an hour up
the mountain she killed a rattlesnake. Nancy got to the ridge and
then rested herself. Then she started to the peak of the cliffs.
She got to the eagle's nest. In it was a newborn baby. She got a
stick and ran the eagle off. She got the baby and headed back
down the mountain. William met her and she told him what
happened. They got off the mountain and all the Naillons and
everybody looked at the baby. No one knew who the baby was.
Nancy raised it. She named him Tom.

Grandma Bertha also told me how Bill Moore lost his leg. He
was trimming a tree. His mule was hooked to a log. Bill was
driving the mule down the hill with the plow lines. Bill slipped
and fell. He rolled down the hill. His leg hit one of the logs that
was piled up down below. His leg was broken. The mule pulled
beside the hill. The log came unhooked and cut Bill's broken leg
almost all the way off. William got his belt and wrapped it around
the stump to stop the bleeding. He got home and a doctor had to
finish cutting the leg off with a meat saw. It took a year for him
to heal.

William Moore and Nancy Cope Moore had a daughter that
they named Nancy Moore. She was born August 4, 1821. Patrick
Naillon and Frances Russell Naillon had a son and named him
Elijah Washington Naillon. He was born October 26, 1826. Elijah
and Nancy were dating and Nancy got with child. She gave him
the Moore name because she had her reasons.

Elijah Washington and Nancy Moore was my great-great-
great grandpa: and grandma. Over the years they went their own
ways. Elijah Washington Naillon had another son, Joseph Reed
Vance Naillon. Elijah W. Naillon had a big family. Nancy meet a
man named William Franklin and had Joseph Moore. She gave
him the Moore name also.

During the Civil War, Elijah Washington Naillon was in the mounted Calvary of Captain G. W. Kirk's Company, 3rd Regiment. He enlisted as a private at Knoxville, Tennessee on July 29, 1864. His personal description was as follows: age fifty; height 5 feet, 11 inches; complexion fair; hair brown; eyes blue.

While a member of the organization aforesaid, in the service and in the line of his duty, at or near a place called Newport, Cocke County, in the State of Tennessee, on or about the 20th day of November 1864 he being at the time on detached service captured a rebel soldier and said Elijah Washington Naillon came home with a rebel prisoner chained by the neck to his mule and after keeping him during the night tied to his own person he took the prisoner as before confined and he started to the federal army via Cocke County Tennese, said soldier claimed to belong to Morgan S. Vaughn's command and Elijah W. Naillon escorting him to Union lines the prisoner took advantage at an unguarded moment to attack him with a stone knocking said Naillon down by striking him upon the head, and after falling repeating the blows until said Naillon was wholly disabled.

After the Civil War, Elijah tried too get a pension. He wrote this letter March 19, 1891. The proof is on file with B. F. Witt of Indianapolis. The letter was published in a Tennessee newspaper June, 27, 1904.

Oh my God, my God, why hast thou forsaken me? I often walk in my yard and look upon my old mossy house and my little farm sold off to raise my helpless children.When I look at the children, plaefaced for want of food and clothing they look like dirt eaters. I think, 'why has my government forgotten me?' My disabilities are such that I have not been able to work since the war. On the 24th of June 1880 I filed a claim being nearly destitute of all the benefits of a solder and left not able to do any work. I now am suffering. All I ask is for the government to give me give me what is just. Please give me your reply as early a day as possible. I hope the Holy Spirit may be your guide.

Elijah died at the Shelby Country Poorhouse. He had been there ever since he had been found by a patrolman wandering around the old depot. His people at Spanish Fork in Utah were notified. A reply was received which stated that his relatives were unable to look after the body. The body was then turned over to the county undertaker with the instruction that his body might be sent to Utah at some future date. Today where great-great-great grandpa Elijah Washington Naillon is buried is a parking lot. All the graves with marked in cement so the people can still find their graves today.

Nancy Moore was the mother of Joseph Moore. Joseph Moore was in the Civil War. Joseph enlisted in the service of the United States at Morristown in the State of Tennessee, on the 20th day of November 1863. He enlisted as a private in Company K, commanded by John Ashbury Fowler in the 8th Regiment of the Tennessee Cavalry volunteers. He died of measles while on duty at Nashville on April 14, 1864. Nancy Moore my great-great grandma got a pension of $8 dollars a month. Nancy died in 1895 and is buried in the Naillon town graveyard.

Nancy Moore and Elijah Washington Naillon had a son, and William Ellijah Moore. He married Sarah Jane Price. William and Sarah are my great-great-grandpa and grandma. They had a daughter named Nancy Ellen Moore. She married William Mack Leatherwood. They had seven children: Chuck, Will, Charlie, Grover, Bertha, Lona, and Judy.

Nancy Ellen Moore and William Mack Leatherwood were my great grandpa and grandma. During the late 1800s my grandma Bertha told me that most of the Naillons left Naillon Town and went out west with the Mormons who practiced polygamy. This was in 1870. Some of the Naillons settled near Bosie, Idaho. They caught wild horses, broke them, and sold them.

Lydia Margaret Naillon, daughter of Elijah Washington also went West with the Mormons. She lived in Utah. Aaron Montgomery Naillon was the son of Elijah and Harriet Naillon. They also went west with the Mormons. They lived near Boise, Idaho, in the 1800s.

Russell Naillon and his son Elijah went to Utah to live with the Mormons. Pauline was the daughter of Lydia Margaret Naillon. Most of the Naillons were Mormons. The Naillons were mountain people. When they first came to Naillon they hunted, fished, trappped, and farmed the land of Naillon Town.

Wiliam Joseph Arrington was born June 12, 1860 and died March 10, 1948. Rachel Norton was born July 7, 1862 and died December 22, 1900. William Joseph Arrington married Rachel Norton April 25, 1880 in Madison, North Carolina where they were born. They had a son named Kelse Natan Arrington who was born in 1895. After the death of his mother Rachel Kelse Natan Arrington left North Carolina to come to what is now called Hartford, Tennessee, in 1910. At that time he was working for Borice Hart Lumber Company as a water boy. He was fourteen years old.

William Mack Leatherwood had a daughter named Bertha. She and Kelse meet one day while William was buying a load of lumber to work on an old barn. Bertha Leatherwood and Kelse Natan Arrington had sixteen children. Bertha was born in 1901. Kelse Natan Arrington come to Tennessee. After dating Bertha for about a year he and Bertha got married in 1917. They lived in Naillon Town. Kelse worked at the lumber company. Bertha had her first child at seventeen. She named him Hugo. He was born October 11, 1917. He had blond hair and blue eyes.

During World War I, influenza was killing people worldwide. The mountain people called it the Super Flu. It killed one in every family in the mountains. The Arrington's were struck with the flu in October 1918. Kelse and Bertha lay flu-sick and could not get out of bed. One-year-old Hugo would carry them water to drink from a bucket with a dipper. Hugo got his toys and put them in a box and said that he was going home. It broke Bertha's and Kelse's heart. Hugo walked a mile down the hollow to the cabin of Nancy and Mack Leatherwood. Bertha's mom and dad and Nancy saw him and went out to get him. They saw that Kelse and Bertha were not with them. Nancy picked him up and placed him on her hip. Mack headed to the cabin of Bertha and Kelse. When he got there and found them sick with the flu. He and Nancy stayed until they got better. Little Hugo took the flu died on November 23, 1918. He was buried at the family graveyard on top of the mountain in Naillon Town, Tennessee.

In 1923 a flood come and washed away the lumberyard in Hartford. After the death of Hugo, Bertha had three more children. They were named Carrine, Elsy, and Frankie. She left and went to Virginia. Nancy and Mack stayed in Naillon Town. Chuck Leatherwood bought a place in Raven Branch. Later on Mack and Nancy Leatherwood moved in.

In 1924 Kelse move back to Tennessee. Bertha was carrying her fifth child. She had her and named her Ruth Ellen Arrington. The Kelse's bought a place in the Old 15th of Cocke County from the Arwoods. Kelse had two five-dollar gold pieces. He used them to buy a 93-acre farm. It had an old house on it that was story and a half. It also had a barn that set above the hill and an old corncrib. It also had and a field that was called the bottom. Ruth Ellen Arrington was born November 17, 1924, after the death of Joyce. This was in October sometime in 1938.

The *Newport Pain Talk* reported that an eleven-year-old boy shot a nine-year-old girl. Funeral services for the Arrington child were conducted from home Monday afternoon with the Reverend Robert Hall in charge. Burial was in the family cemetery.

When World War II broke out most of the young men went to the army. After the war, Albert Morrow came to the Old 15th County in Del Rio where he was rased. He married Ruth Ellen Arrington in 1947. William Mack Leatherwood was born January 22, 1869 and died on January 8, 1943. Nancy Ellen Moore

Leatherwood born July 1877 and died February 25, 1963. Nancy and William Leatherwood were my great grandma and grandpa.

Bertha Leatherwood was born July 12, 1901 and died March 4, 1986. Kelse Natan Arrington born March 29, 1885 and died in August of 1973. Bertha and Kelse are buried at the old family graveyard near the Valley View Church in the Old 15th County. All Bertha Leatherwood kinfolks on the Naillon's side were Mormons. Kelse Natan Arrington kinfolks were Church of God. They use to go to Grapevine Church of God in Madison, North Carolina.

After Kelse and Bertha were married they joined the old Pigeon Valley Baptist Church on Mill Creek in Hartford, Tennessee. Kelse and Bertha Arrington were farmers most of their life. My father, Albert Morrow, and most of his people came from Mack Patch, North Carolina. My great-great grandpa Albert Morrow was born in 1820 and married Judy Firsbee in 1840. They had a son named Charle Morrow in 1850. He married Judy Davis. Their children were Ida, Arkie, London, Charlie, and twins, Tommy and Rachel. Rachel never grew much and she died at the age of twelve years old. All of Charle and Judly Davis Morrow's children were born in the late 1800s.

This was told to be by Aunt Vick. My great-great grandpa Albert Morrow got shot off the back of a white mule for saying that he was a tar hill. The man that shot my great-great grandpa said that he had killed his best friend. Albert was buried on Poplar Gap in an old graveyard.

Charle and Judy Davis Morrow were my great grandpa and grandma. Their son Tommy came to Del Rio, Tennessee. He was born 1883 in Mack Patch, North Carolina. Bertie Fish was the daughter of Lawson Fish and Lou Allen Russell. Bertie Fish and my father Albert Morrow are the people that Catherine Marshall wrote about in the book, *Christy*.

John Fish died July 1, 1861. He came to America from England with his brother Jim. They came on a ship loaded with horses. The ship sank before they reached land. John and Jim along with the rest of the survivor swam the rest of the way to land holding onto the horses. John settled in to Crab Tree, North Carolina, and his brother Jim settled in Kentucky. John met and married Nancy Lowe. John got killed in the war in July 1861, when his youngest child, Fidella Clingman, was six months old. Both John and Nancy Lowe Fish are said to be buried at Crab Tree close to a Church of God. They were of the Church of God faith. They were my great-great grandpa and grandma. John Fish's wife was one-quarter Indian, Their children were William and Marion Fish, born February 18, 1845, Lawson Fish born in 1850, and then they had other children named Sarah, Lizzie, Lottie, Ath, and Fidella Clingman Fish.

William Marion Fish got married February 23, 1865 at Fines Creek in Haywood County, North Carolina, to Laura Aualine Griffith. She was born May 9, 1847. During that time Lawson Fish married Lou Ellen Russell. Lawson and Lou Ellen were my great grandpa and grandma. William Marion and Lawson Fish were sheep ranchers and farmers in Fines Creek, North Carolina, eighteen years before moving to Cocke County, Tennessee, in 1883. Their home was on the head of Fines Creek in front of Hebow Mountain. They moved to Tennessee on a wagon by the way of Max Patch. They brought their sheep, which were branded. One of the sheep left Tennessee and returned to Fines Creek, a distance of many miles. They crossed round the mountain, down Danevilles to the Old 15th, and into Chapel Hollow. William Marion Fish and Lawson Fish and their family stopped at the Clicks and later on through the mountain. They came to the old Rockie Top road and over to the farm that was located on about 400 arces of land in the Old 15th district of Cocke County at the foot of Rocky Top. The land was later sold to Fred O'Dell. He sold the land to a man named Danny. Lawson Fish and Lou Ellen Russell Fish had several children. Their names of their children were Aldin, Ira Bascum, Cas, Robert Lee, Della, Mattie, Baxter, and Bertie.

William Fances Click married Cora Fish, James Newton Click married Alice Fish. Marion Stephen Click married Marcilia Fish. The Clicks was brothers and the Fish sister was the daughter of William Marian Fish and Laura Aualine Griffith. It was the Clicks that gave the land for the mission in the book *Christy* that Catherine Marshall wrote.

Tommy Morrow met Bertie in the Old 15th and they got married in 1915. They moved to Huff Hollow. Bertie Fish Morrow and Tommy Morrow had nine children. The first two, Robert and Harlie, died when at birth. Both were buried in the Arrington and Morrow graveyard in Catgut in Cocke County.

This is how Bertie and little Fiffie died. August 6, 1930 was hot and muggy. The hot air blew through the open door of the cabin that lead to the bedroom where Bertie was laying in pain for the child to be born. Tommy and the rest of the children, Walter, Victoria, Jodie, and Albert, were on their knees praying for her. A midwife was there to help with the birth. Zora was the oldest and she was helping her mother. The baby came out. The midwife got the baby and washed it and gave it to Bertie. It was lying in her arms. There was a look and longing of love in Bertie eyes that night as she looked at her newborn baby. She told Zora to come close. Bertie kissed Zora on the forehead and told her that she loved her. She thanked the midwife for helping her. Little Fiffie took the fever and a doctor was sent for. When he got there and he told Tommy that Bertie and the baby had what they call child birth fever. He said that they would not make it. Three days later Effie was dead. Tommy had to get a coffin maker to make a coffin. The name of the coffin maker was Trent. It broke Tommy's heart when he took the dead baby from Bertie and placed it in the coffin. He nailed the lid shut on the coffin. Walter and some of the kinfolks dug a grave in Catgut at the Morrow and Arrington graveyard. Tommy carried the coffin to the grave on the hill and buried little Effie. That night Bertie burnt up with the fever. She burnt all night with the fever Tommy laid a white rag on her head and wet it with cold water every half hour. They use oil lamps for light. Tommy sat in an old wooden chair holding his wife's hand as he looked through the window of the bedroom cabin. The moon had come full over the pine trees and was shining down on the cabin. The moon light ran through the window on the old cabin floor. The moonlight shone on Bertie and she told her family goodbye. She told Tommy that she loved him. She died the following day. She was put in a coffin and hauled to the Catgut graveyard on a sleigh pulled buy a mule. She was laid to rest. That night Albert, her eight-year-old son, saw his mother came back in a ghostly shadow. She told him to be good and that he could be with her some day. Albert followed her back to the graveyard. It was a full moon and when she got to the grave she vanished.

The *Newport Plain Talk* of May 5, 1935 reported that Walter Morrow's son, Mr. Tommy Morrow of the 15th was fatally injured about nine o'clock Saturday morning when the wheels of a heavily loaded 2-ton truck passed over his body. He died at McGowan Hospital in Jefferson City Saturday night at 9:00 P.M. Funeral services were held in the home on Monday afternoon at two. The family pastor was in charge. Walter was buried it the Morrow cemetery in Catgut.

In 1936 Zora left and married a man named Clark. She was gone nearly a year. Tommy did not know where she was. She came back home in 1936. She was with child and died that fall from tuberculosis. She was buried beside her brother Walter in the Morrow cemetery. She was eighteen years old.

After he got back from the war in 1943, Albert Morrow married Ruth Ellen Arrington, the daughter of Kelse and Bertha Arrington. They moved on Raven Branch in Del Rio. They had three children, Iom, Jean, and Donald. While there, a windstorm came and Albert let the mule out of the barn. The storm blew the barn down and it blew the house off its foundation.

In 1953 Abert and Ruth and the children moved to Ohio. Albert worked in the steel mill. One day a pipe broke and the steam from the pipe knocked him out. He told me that it took months to get over it. While there, Albert's wife got with child. She was going to the doctor while Albert was at work. She called a cab. She got into the cab. Donald and Iom Jean got in with her. When they got to the doctor's office, it was on the other side of the streets. Donald jumped out of the cab and started to run.

There was car a coming. Ruth saw in a vision an angel come down and pick him up and set him on the other side of the street where the doctor office was. The cab driver asked Ruth if she had seen that and she said, "Yes, sir."

Wanda was born on April 8, 1954. That fall they left Ohio and moved back to Raven Branch. On March 6, 1955 I, James E. Morrow, was born. Albert sold out at Raven Branch and move to Roda Bell Coggins' place. The only way to the cabin was around the cliff or twice through the creek to get there. There was no light or running water in the houses backs them. We uses outside bathrooms, called moon houses. I took sick with worms and liked to die.

Donald and Iom Jean had to walk around the cliff to go to the Bell Hill schoolhouse. One day as they were coming him from school, Donald walked over a big copperhead. Iom Jean liked to step on it. I got worse sick with worms. I had a blue blanket that I would not let anyone touch. Old Doc Fish come and gave me some medicine. He said time would tell. Ruth told Albert if I did not make it she was going to bury me in the blue blanket. Mom lay down beside me and morning come and I was up crawling around. Albert and Ruth and the children moved to High Point, North Carolina. We started to school at Oak Hill School. While there mom got with child. She had miscarriage and was taken to the hospital. She was in a coma for seven days and lost much blood. When she woke up, she told us that while in the coma she was at this place that she said was beautiful land and she was at peace and she had no worries and pain and the land was bright and fair. She said she wanted to stay but Jesus told her that she had children and had to go back and care for to them until grown and then you can come back home and be at peace. She woke up and a colored woman was fixing her hair. She got her strength back and she got with child again. His name was Timothy W. Morrow. Benny and Susie were born at the old Roda Bell Coggins place in Tennessee. In 1963 dad got to drinking heavily and my mom left him. In 1965 and we stayed with grandpa and grandma Bertha and Kelse for a while. We moved into a three-room house that

belonged to uncle Johnny Shelton. We farmed there, Albert
come back, and he and mom got back together. Daddy bought me
a pony and we later moved on the old Ikie Raine farm. We had
two cows, hogs, and two ponies. One was half pony and half horse.
One evening after working on the farm my cousin, Edward
Frisbee on the Fish side and Randy Laws and I were riding horses.
My horse fell through the bridge that had a rotted plank in it. I
broke my hip and was taken to Knoxville hospital. I was there July
to November. I was put in a cast from my chest to my feet. It
was nearly a year before I could walk and it left my leg 3 inches
shorter them the other. This happened in 1969.

My daddy's father, Thomas Morrow, died December 28,
1968. He was married to his fourth wife at the time, Sarah Teague
Morrow. He was buried in the Union graveyard in Newport,
Tennessee. I was fighting roosters at that time. Daddy had got to
drinking again and Ruth left him again.

While we were raising tomatoes at uncle Jerry Green's place
a boy shot the mule and killed my pony. Later on we bought the
old Frank Stokely place cross the creek down below the Ikie
Raine place. That was in 1970. In 1972 a flood came and washed
everything away. That morning the Lord woke Mom and she told
us we could not get to school. It had been raining for days and
that morning the big creek was coming down and it washed the
bridge away. It washed our barn away, even the cows. A young girl
got washed away in Hartford. It washed the old Turner barn away
and washed holes in the fields so big that you could bury houses in
them. Acres were washed away. It was the biggest flood sense
1943 that washed grandpa Button away.

In 1975 I repented of my sins and started to live for Jesus.
Lester Raines moved back in from New Jersey. I was going to a
Baptist church at the time. At Sunday school the teacher was
reading the sixteenth chapter Mark. He got to where they shall
took up serpents. He said that some churches do handle serpents
in their church. He said if you believe you can, too. He said the
Baptist did not practice serpent handling. In the fall of 1977 we
were hanging tobacco and I saw a copperhead lying on a red clay

bank. I caught it and put in a box. The next day Lester was at his house. He was lying on the bed. He had sugar real bad. He told me to set the box with the copperhead in it on a small table that was near his bed. He prayed to Jesus and opened the box. He reached into it and pulled the copperhead out by the tail. It crawled up his arm. He was saying, "thank you sweet Jesus" over and over. The serpent just lay there. About that time his son, Gene Raines, came in with a big black copperhead in a box. The anointing fell on me. I opened the box, reached in and got the big black copperhead. Gene also handled it. The copperhead that Lester that was handling crawled off his arm and went back into the box. Lester was a great man of God and had more faith them anyone that I know. He would preach and when the anointing would come he would handle serpents. That same year Lester Raines passed on and was buried at the Moore graveyard. His funeral service was at Sand Hill. Liston Pack held the service and I was a pall bearer.

In 1978 I meet Pamela Ford. She lived down at the old Pierce place that her grandpa owned. We got to going together in April. We dated, too. July 8 was a Saturday and I came down and asked Pamela if she wanted to get married. We already had the papers to get married with. That evening before church we left early and headed to Pastor Marvin Turner's house. At that time he was living with his mother, Mary Turner. We got there and asked if he would marry us. He told us to come on in. His wife, Jo Ann, was talking to Pamela. Pamela's friend, Tammy Reece, was with us. He married us. We told him that we were going on to Sand Hill Church of God in Jesus' Name. Bonnie and John Ike came to church with us. After church we went back to their house and stayed the night.

I rented a three-room house. It had no water. It had an outside bathroom or the moon house or the Johnny house. People called them many things back them. We got moved. We carried water to drink and cook with from the spring across the road at old springhouse. We lived by a creek. Pamela and I would go to the creek after I came in from work at a log cabin company. We would go swimming. By the fall of the year she was with child. In November of 1978, we moved back in with Bonnie and John Ike Ford.

In late February of 1979, a horrible snowstorm moved in. The snow was knee deep. When the storm broke, John and I was getting wood. That night Pamela was hurting. I tried to get her to go to the doctor. However, the room temperature dropped down to zero and the road were iced over. Pamela got too hurting real bad. I got the car started. I let it was warm up and then got Pamela into the car. John Ike and Bonnie got into the car with us. We had to go up Stokely Hill. The ice on the road was so slick that I slid off the road. We all got out of the car. Pamela started hemorrhaging. I carried her up Stokely Hill. The air was so cold it hurt your lungs as you breathed. John Ike helped carry Pamela down the hill. When we got to Walter's house we called for help. They sent a four-wheel drive out and took us on to the hospital. Pam miscarried. She had to stay in the hospital. Her sister, Jean, and Neil came and took Bonnie and John Ike home. Neil gave me twenty dollars. In a few days Pamela was out of the hospital.

Spring came. In 1979 we farmed and raised tobacco and in the year 1980 we farmed and raises tobacco again. In the fall Pamela and I were gathering pumpkins. We were loading them on a sleigh pulled by a pony that we bought from Curly Stokely. John Ike came up and told us that Bonnie's father, Robert Lee Pierce, was dead. We came on in. I stopped at the barn. I unhitched the pony and turned it back in to the pasture. I unloaded the pumpkins and come into the house. They had his funeral. Robert Lee Pierce was laid to rest beside his wife, Eliza Clark Pierce, in the Union graveyard in Newport in Cocke County, Tennessee.

That same year we moved to Chapel Hollow where Opal Myers owned land. We moved into the old Click cabin. This is where all my ancestors, the Fish family and the Click family, had lived. These are the people that Catherine Marshall wrote about in the book *Christy*.

The first night in the old Click cabin Pamela and I slept on a mattress on the floor. The next morning I woke up and there was a house snake lying beside the mattress on the floor. I got up and got the snake and put him outside. We moved the bed upstairs.

We had a spring on the outside to get water to cook with and drink. This is the same cabin Leonora Whitaker came too when aunt Marcilia Fish Click lived here in 1912. It had an outside bathroom.

One night while sleeping upstairs, a big black snake fell in bed with us. Pamela jumped up. I got the snake and went downstairs and threw it out the front door.

Winter was coming on and we had to go to the woods and cut trees and pull them down with the horses and ponies. We cut the trees up and stacked the logs for the winter months. The fist Thanksgiving that we lived in the old Click house we had a turkey baking. The ceiling caught on fire where the stovepipe ran through the roof of the house. We had to get water and put it out. We had the Thanksgiving dinner cooked and we had a good diner.

While we lived there, I hauled the children to school in the morning. I had an old mule that I ploughed with at the old Pierce place. The mule died and we had to put him in Old Hollow above the old barn. At night wild animals would come and eat on the dead mule until he was gone and nothing but bones was left.

In 1981 an old preacher came to the chapel telling people that he was going to build the mission back, but he never did. He was trying to get the land for himself. I went to help him one morning. He told me that the mission would never be built back. Somehow, he got the deed in his name. That same year Pamela and I moved back in the house we lived in when we were first married. In the early 1950s the Lord spoke to Robert Fraley and his wife Mary. The Lord told them to go to Norton, Virginia, and to pray for Ben Johnson. They did and he got better. The Lord healed him.

During that time at the church, it was a man name Mullins. Rattlesnakes at that time were huge. Most rattlesnakes that you caught were as big as a man's arm. Most were 5 foot and sometimes 6 foot long. During a service Roscoe Mullins got a large rattlesnake out and it bit him; it was a bad bite. The rattlesnake's fangs went deep into the flesh of Roscoe's hand. When the rattlesnake turned loose it was put in the box. Roscoe's hand had started to swell. He was taken home to get better. As the days went by, his hand turned black and blue. It began to hurt all the time and get no better. Mullins sought medical attention and the hand and part of his arm was amputated below his elbow.

In 1955 Pelfrey had been arrested for handling a serpent but the law let him go and nothing ever came of it. Over the years the Holiness Church of God in Jesus' Name at Big Stone Gap, Virginia, and the Church of God in Jesus' Name at Del Rio, Tennessee handled serpents. The Wells, Kilgores, Spears, Cliftons, Sturgills, Smiths, and Oscar Pelfery were associated with the headquarter church in Big Stone Gap. The Turners, Raines, James, Packs, and the Balls went to the Sand Hill Church of God in Jesus' Name in Del Rio, Tennessee.

The first time that anybody got bit at the Sand Hill Church of God in Jesus' Name it happened like this. That day before the church service five boys went to a man's farm. They were cursing him, calling him bad names. They tore down his fence. That night, before the church service got started, Mullins from Virginia brought a huge serpent; it was nearly 6 feet long. Aunt Glady Fish McMahan, Uncle Oll McMahan and Oscar Franklin Palfrey and his family also came from Virginia. Outside, before service, someone showed Edward Lee the serpent. It was the biggest one that he ever saw. Blackburn brought it into the church and set it on the bench up front. A boy standing in the church said he could handle that big snake if he did not sin today. One of the boys that was with him told a man, "If he does he will get bit." This was because what they done that day at the man's farm. As the service got started, Blackburn got out two copperheads and handled them. He put them up and reached in another box and got the huge rattlesnake out. He was handling it and when the boy came and got it. As the boy was handling it, the huge snake wrapped around his neck. Then it crawled down his arm and the rattlesnake bit him on the hand. In just in a few minutes the boy sank to the floor of the church. The faithful started to pray for him. Glady and Oll McMahan started to pray for him. People started to leave the church. They got in their cars and left at a high rate of speed out of the hollow in the Old 15th. Three dogs were run over that night. A man told me that the next morning there were three dogs laying dead as you go out the Old 15th

Some people remained at the church. A man was cursing and swearing. He was saying words that only a bad person says. He said he was going to call the law. He did and the boy was taken to the doctor. He was put in hospital. That day the law come up and found the snakes that were lying in their boxes outside in the high weeds behind the church. They arrested Euel Jacky Blackburn. It was eight days later before the boy got to feel better. They gave Backburn six months in the workhouse. After doing his time in the workhouse, he went back in to Virginia. He had sugar. One late evening, he blacked out and fell in a ditch. He was found the next day by kinfolks. He was about frozen to death. He was speaking in tongues; he was trying to tell them something. He was taken to the hospital.

Blackburn lived in a cabin. One night he had a big fire in the stove. While he was asleep the house caught on fire and burnt the cabin down while he was in it. The following day Euel Blackburn found his remains. He was buried somewhere in Virginia.

Blackburn had a half-brother in Tennessee named Miller. This was in the late fifties. Some say Blackburn went into a sugar coma and died, also. Over the months while Euel Jacky Blackburn was in jail, the people from the church would go to see him on Sundays. He would sing to them from his jail cell. At that time, the jail was in the courthouse as it is today. The Worley Ball family would come out of the old Fish place that was in the head of Cool Branch and out to the main road and down the 15th to Del Rio and on into Newport to see Blackburn in jail. On Sundays he preached and sang as they stood in the courthouse yard. His children were small at the time but they remember him sitting at the windows with bars on it.

# Chapter 18

"A voice is heard in Ramah, Rachel weeping and great mourning, Rachel weeping for her children and refusing to be comforted, because they are no more." (Matthew 2:18)

## The Family Tree of Pamela Ford

Joseph Alexander Ford was born in 1775 in England. He and his brother John Tipton Ford came to America about the turn of the eighteenth century. They split up on their arrival, each traveling in different a direction. Joseph Ford married Sarah McMullen and reared a family of thirteen in Burke County, North Carolina. Benjamin Jackson and Tipton and James Ford came to Tennessee and settled in the Cocke County area. Benjamin Jackson Ford's family disapproved of his marriage to Nancy Mantooth because she was part Cherokee Indian. Benjamin Jackson Ford and Nancy Mantooth were Pamela Gail Ford's great-great grandpa and grandma. The disapproval of their marriage by their family motivated Benjain and Nancy to leave North Carolina and go to Tennessee.

Benjamin Jackson Ford was born 1805. Nancy Mantooth was born 1817. They were married on May 24, 1836. Nancy Mantooth was the daughter of John Lillard and Lettie Virginia Mantooth. Lettie Virgina or Jeannie Mantooth was a full-blooded Cherokee Indian. Benjamin Jackson and Nancy Ford lived in a log house on grassy fork near Snow Bird Mountain. Benjamin and Nancy had thirteen children. Their names were Sarah, Anna Jane, James Lewis, Nancy Evenly, Margaret Lizzie, Elizabeth,

Joseph, Mary Polly, Lettie Cordelia, Reuben Tipton, Issac, John, and Lillard Ford.

The first son of Nancy and Benjamin Jackson Ford was John Ford, Sr. John Ford, Sr., was born 1837. His first wife was Roda Ranies. She was born August 14, 1937, and died in September 1888. Roda Raines could have been the sister to my uncle, Ikeie Raines. After the death of Roda, John married Llizzie Willis. John Ford and Lizzie Willis were Pamela Gail Ford's great grandpa and grandma. The children of John Ford and Lizzie Willis Ford were Charlie, Ralph, Tilson, Posey, and Lewis Ford. Benjamin Jackson Ford died in 1890. He was buried at the Mt. Zion Graveyard at Grassy Fork. Nancy Mantooth died 1907 and was buried at the same place beside her husband.

This story was told to me by John Ike Ford the great grandson of Nancy Mantooth and Benjamin Ford. It was also by Pamela's daddy. The time that Benjamin Jackson Ford and Nancy Mantooth Ford settled in Grassy Fork at the foot of Snow Bird Mountain the valley was infested with rats. They would get in the corncrib and eat the corn. In those days there were plenty of rattlesnakes. They would catch rats. In the head of Snow Bird Mountain was one of the largest dens of rattlesnakes in these parts of Cocke County. Benjamin John, his oldest son, would go to the den and take two potato sacks and a stick with a rope fixed on it to put round the rattlesnakes. He would pull the rope tight. As one person caught the rattlesnake, the other would hold the sack to put it in. When they would catch five or six rattlesnakes they would come back off Snow Bird Mountain. The rattlesnakes would lay in the cracks of the cabin and soon the rat populating began to die out as the rattlesnake would kill them and eat them. The rattlesnakes would stay during the feeding months and head back to the den in the fall of the year.

Isaac Greenville Ford was born January 25, 1865. He was the youngest of thirteen children. Benjamin Jack Ford was a farmer who was known to drink moonshine, which was readily available in that area. When Isaac was old enough to persuade his dad

Benjamin to give up drinking. Benjamin quit and never drank again.

Benjamin and Nancy raised thirteen children on the fertile and rocky farm at Grassy Fork. Isaacs married Cynthia Jane Smith on January 6, 1884. Cynthia Jane Smith was born March 11, 1867. Cynthia Jane Smith and Isaac Greenville Ford were Pamela Gail Ford's great grandpa and grandma. Isaac Ford was a farmer, schoolmaster, music teacher, and song leader at Mt. Zion Church. During World War II, at the age of eighty-two, he was asked and consented to return to Grassy Fork School and teach during the shortage of teachers. He also served on the board of tax assessment in Newport for several years. He was an inspiration and encouragement to all who knew him. Isaac and Cynthia Jane Ford lived in a house that was build about 1888, shortly after their second child was born. Their new home was build a few feet from the old log home was that was torn down.

Some of the logs were used to build the kitchen onto the new frame house. The smoke house was located about 30 feet behind the new home. It was also built with logs from the old house. Isaac and Cynthia brought his mother and dad into their home where they cared for them until their deaths.

It was at this house that they reared their nine children. The children of Isaac Greenville Ford and Cynthia Jane Smith were Ida, Lena, Algie, Lora, Eve Evaline, Ernest, Ben, and Corda. All of them are now deceased. They also raised Lora Jane the daughter of their son, Benjamin Natan Ford. Lora Janes's mother, Lora Presnell Ford, died when she gave birth to Lora Jane. John Ford, Sr., died in 1934. Lizzie Willis Ford died in 1938.

Isaac Greenville Ford was also a coffin maker. He died April 18, 1954. His wife Cynthia Jane Smith died April 6, 1956. All these people are buried in the Mt. Zion graveyard in Cocke County at Grassy Fork, Tennessee. The reason that both brothers were Pamela Gail Ford great grand pas and grandmas is that their children Eve Evaline Ford the daughter of Isaac Greenville Ford and Cynthia Jane Smith Ford, married the son of John Ford, Sr., and Lizzie Willis Ford. Posey Rufus Ford married his first cousin Evaline Ford. Eva Evaline Ford was born September 4, 1899. She was the daughter of Isaac Greenville Ford and Cynthia Smith. Posey Ford was born April 24, 1901 in Cocke County, Tennessee. He was the son of John Ford and Lizzie Willis. Posey Rufus Ford and Evaline Ford were married January 24, 1919. Their children were John, Ike, Ted, Fred, William, Mary, Lizzie, Cynthia, Lorine, Leona Villa, and Charles Roe. All these children except one were born on Grassy Fork. Ted ford was born in Cold Spring, North Carolina. He died as a baby and was buried there. While Evaline Ford and Posey Ford lived in the Old 15th, their children were named John, Fred, Lizzie, Lorine, Leona, and Charles Roe. They lived in an old cabin that set across the creek. They had an old iron kettle and the boys would fill it with water. After that they would build a fire and get the water boiling. Then the boys would go and cut poke salad. Eva Evaline would boil it and feed it to the hogs.

While they lived in Grassy Fork they had daughter named Mary. She was born in April 1926 but died and was buried at the old Mount Zion graveyard on Grassy Fork. Fred told his sister, Lizzie that they were having a meeting in the old Zion church house. An old man was preaching. When he came to the end of the sermon he gave an altar call. John Ike Ford went up in his old overalls and white shirt. He was barefoot and got down on his knees and asked Jesus to forgive him. He was saved that day.

Posey Rufus Ford was also a coffin maker. He lived in the old 15th. in a log cabin across the creek. Pamela Ford's aunt Lizzie Cynthia told this story. This happened at the foot of Snow Bird Mountain. Frank Ford and Sada Ford were sharecroppers on the Parker Ford farm. One of the coldest winters was in 1936. It snowed heavily. The creeks and the ponds of waters and the mountain streams froze over. Frank and Kennth were getting wood. They were dragging it across the frozen pond. Kennth slipped, hit his head, and knocked himself out. The oxen pulled the logs to the woodyard at the cabin. Frank found Kennth on the ice. His head was still bleeding. Over the months his head become swollen. He never got over hitting his head and he died nine months later. He was buried on Grassy Fork in a coffin Posey made. It was lined with white cloth this was the last coffin that Posey ever made. If the child dies they are buried in a white coffin; if a grown person dies they are buried in a black coffin.

Eva Evaline Ford died on December 12, 1961 in Fulton, Georgia. Posey Rufus Ford died May 2, 1951 in Jefferson County, Tennessee. He is buried at the Union graveyard in Newport, Tennessee.

Most of the Fords were Baptist. The Mt. Zion Baptist Church was founded June 4, 1853 at Grassy Fork, Tennessee, at Cocke County. It was a log church. A fire destroyed the first church. A heavy blanket of snow in the winter of 1901–1902 caused the roof of the second church to collapse. One half of the church building went flying into the creek. The pulpit was the only thing that was not damaged. A decision was made and the member sold the church property. The church was moved a mile and a half up the road. Ben Henderson donated the land for the new church. This was the third church and is still standing today on the hill at Grassy Fork.

Pamela Ford's great grandpa on the Clark side was William Bill Clark. His first wife was Louisa Lou Nichols. He and Louisa had seven children. Pamela Ford's ancestors told this story. It happened nearly 300 years ago. It was told to Eliza Clark, Pamela's grandma and; it was also told to Pamela' mother Bonnie Pierce Ford. She told it to Pamela. It is part of mountain folklore. Bill Clark's first wife, Louisa Nichols had many ancestors who have lived and died before us. They were born in the late 1700s. They may have been part Indian, as they were known to keep company with the Cherokees. We do not now know if they were miners and actually searched for gold and silver or if they were just fortunate to discover a silver mine. It evidently was not their lifestyle to share what they found with others. Therefore they became greedy. Despite their better judgment they started to make the silver into money or silver coins. The name of the place where the counterfeiting was done was Middle Fork Knob, somewhere in East Tennessee or North Carolina. Things went

good for a while. Then one day someone got to look at a coin
among the other money they had. It did not look exactly right.
There was a dent in the eagle's eye. This had gone unnoticed by
the counterfeiters. The state law officials were told and a search
began for the people responsible. After a long and rugged
manhunt, the persons were spotted in the deep timber forest.
They were not working alone. Cherokee friends were helping
them. When they saw the law coming, they picked up a half-
bushel tub full of silver nuggets and started running. After being
ran after until they could go no farther, they threw the silver
nuggets off a cliff into the water at the bend of the river. The
Cherokee got away. However the Nichols were caught. They
were convicted for counterfeiting money and died in prison.

William Bill Clark lived on Bulls Mountain in Del Rio. He
owned the land that was above his house. That is where he buried
his first wife Louisa Nichols. After the death of Louisa William
married Ellen Cole, Robert Lemon Green told me this story
about her. Ellen Cole was the sister of Hardin Smith Cole. Their
father and mother both died with cancer. Robert was the
grandson of Hardin and Hardin was the brother to Ellen. He
married Sarahbella Leonora Jane Haney and they had a daughter
named Margaret Cole. She married James Robert Green. They
had a son his name who was Robert Lemi Green. The father and
mother of James R. Green was Anderson Green and Eliza Barner.
Robert Lemon Green remembers walking to the church with
Sarahbella, his grandma on the Cole side. The church was built
up high on poles and the lower side. Robert said you could walk up
under the church it was so high off the ground. It was called the
Sandy Gap Church of God. It was built in 1850. It use to sit way
back on the mountain up above the Clark graveyard. William Bill
Clark and Ellen Cole had twelve children. William and Ellen Cole
were Pamela Ford's great grandpa and grandma. It was said that
William Bill Clark fought in the Civil War. He was for the
Union. All Pamela's and my kinfolks fought for the Union.
Nearly two years later some of my ancestors and a friend of theirs
decided to go looking for the lost silver mine. They searched

most of the summer. One day while exploring they came upon a spot about the size of a washtub, where the earth had falling in. They thought it had been a pit of some kind. It appeared to have been filled in with tree limbs, leaves and other forest matter, they said one to the other, "Why not dig here?" The longer they dug, the more excited they became. Six or seven feet down they found tools, such as mattock, shovels and so on. All had the handles rotted away. In the same pit they found human bones and a money mold with a bent in the eagle's eye.

The old house of William and Louisa Clark is gone today. They had nineteen children. Their old house use to stand in the shadow of a high hill. On top of that hill is the Clark Cemetery where William Bill Clark's two wives are laid to rest. He gave that land for a cemetery. Louisa may have been the first to bury there. The tombstones have their birth and death dates as follows: William Bill Clark, 1838–1919; Louisa Clark, 1840–1884; and Ellen Cole Clark, 1859–1941.

William Bill Clark and Ellen Cole Clark had a daughter. They named her Eliza. Eliza Cark married Robert Lee Pierce. They had eleven children: Bonnie, Clyde, Curtis, Tory, Helen, Fain, Dorothy, Anna Lee, Earl, Corral, and Mammie.

Eliza Clark and Robert Lee Pierce are Pamela's grandpa and grandma. Henry Clayton Pierce was born March 26, 1835 and died November 8, 1891 at the age of fifty-six. Charlotte Cogdill Pierce was the wife of Henry Clayton Pierce. Charlotte was born June 1844 and died April 1916. Henry and Charlotte were Pamela's great-great grandpa and grandma on the Pierce side.

Henry Clayton Pierce and Charlotte Cogdill Pierce were father and mother of Thomas Stonewall Jackson Pierce. Thomas married Margaret Massey. Their five children were Robert Lee, Hester, Lizzie, Rebekah, and Gertrude. Margaret Massey Pierce died at the age of twenty-seven. Thomas Stonewall Jackson Pierce married Laura Ruff after the death of Margaret Massey Pierce. Their nine children were Frances, Bernie, Frank, Daniel, Dewey, Eveline, Plaz, Lottie, and Henrietta. Pamela's grandpa was Robert Lee Pierce. Robert meet Eliza Clark on Bull

Mountain in Del Rio, Tennessee, and married her in 1916. They moved to Lawrence, South Carolina, for two years. They moved to Knox County, Tennessee. Bonnie Kate Pierce was born February 18, 1919. Robert Lee, Eliza and Bonnie moved back to Del Rio, in Cocke County, Tennessee, in 1924 or 1925. They bought the old Penland place. Bonnie Kate Pierce Ford learned that Mel Turner just moved out of his log cabin. The cabin had a long porch on it. Inside the cabin, it had a set of stairs in the middle of the room with had handrails on each side of the stair well. In the closet were two big dolls. Bonnie was five years old at the time she found the dolls. They where the finest things that Bonnie every saw. She got them out the closet and held on to them. She played and slept with them every day. At that time there were plenty of snakes lying around. One day, Robert Lee was working out in the field, Eliza was doing housework, and Bonnie was playing with her big dolls. The old cabin was chinked with red clay and mud. It had a rock foundation. The chimney was mortared with rock and mud. As Bonnie was playing upstairs and she saw a big red rat snake lying on the floor. Bonnie cried and howled because she saw the snake. Eliza comes running upstairs. Eliza told Bonnie to come to her and jump over the rat snake. Bonnie jumped over the snake. Eliza got Bonnie in her arms and was holding her. Bonnie was a crying and said she wanted her dolls. She said, "Mommie, the snake bit my dolls." When Robert Lee came in about noon for dinner, Eliza told him there was a big red rat snake lying on the floor upstairs. He went outside and got a hoe. He went upstairs and killed the snake. He chopped the head off with the hoe. He carried the dead snake down the stairs on the hoe handle. It was 6 foot long and as big round as a man's arm. Robert Lee and Bonnie walked up to the barn with the snake on the hoe handle to the old hog pen. Robert Lee threw the dead snake into the hog pen and the hogs ate it. As he was standing at the hog pen and the hogs were eating the dead snake, Robert Lee was chewing tobacco. He spit tobacco juice into the hog's eyes and the hogs would shake their heads and scream and holler to the top of their lungs.

Robert Lee Pierce and Eliza Clark Pierce farmed all their lives. Robert Lee died on May 23, 1980. He was born August 16, 1888. Eliza Clark Pierce was born October 26, 1899 and died in September, 1871. Both are buried in the Union cemetery. Most of the Pierce's are buried at the old Jonestown graveyard in Jonestown in Del Rio, Tennessee.

Uncle Frank Pierce told this. One night as Thomas Pierce was sleeping a man came to the corncrib and stole some corn. Early next mooring Thomas got up to milk the cow. As he went to the crib to get some corn he saw a plank tore off and corn missing. After he completed his daily work on the farm, he got a fox trap. He wrapped it in old rags and put it in the corncrib. The same man came back and stuck his hand in the corn cab and got his hand caught. He stayed there all night. The next morning Thomas got up and saw the man with his hand in the trap. He said, "Hi," and got his milking done. The he got the man's hand out of the trap and told him come to the house. They ate the early morning meal. Thomas told him, "If you want corn ask me." Thomas gave him a sack of corn and the man went home.

John Ike Ford, the son of Posey and Evaline Ford, was born July 17, 1920. He met Bonnie Kate Pierce, daughter of Robert Lee Eliza Clark Pierce. John Ike and Bonnie Kate got married on August 7, 1943, by the late John Denton at the Cock County Court house in Newport Tennessee. Their first child was Francis Imogene, born May 28, 1945; their second child was Elizabeth Ann Born on April 13, 1948; and their third child was Pamela Gail Ford, born August 20, 1960. All were born in Del Rio. Pamela was born on Round Mountain at the old Wilburn Allen place.

John Ike Ford was in World War II. After the war Bonnie and he farmed. Back then they share cropped with other people. They moved from place to place. While farming with one man, John told me that the tobacco was ready to be cut. The man that owned the farm told John that he had to move. John told the man that he made the tobacco crop and he had a family to feed. The man never said anything else to John. John moved to the old Dave Carver's place. He farmed there one year. Then he moved to the old Pierce farm. He got down sick while he was farming there. In his last days he was taken to Johnson City. He went into a sugar coma and died there. They had his funeral at Brown Chapel Funeral Home. Wayne Haney held the service. John was buried in the Union graveyard. Bonnie stayed with us after the death of John. She moved out a year later. Later she broke her hip and she had to be put in Mariner Health at Newport.

# People who Provided Information for Pam's and My Family Trees

1. Information on the Naillon-Moore-Leatherwood family was given to me by the following persons: Nancy Moore Leatherwood; Bertha Leatherwood Arrington; Beverly Leatherwood, Las Vegas, Nevada; Geraldine F. Griesel, Windsor, Colorado; Geraldine Suckocki Howes, Cave, New York; and Janette Leatherwood Laws.

2. Information on the Arrington: Kelse Natan Arrington, Bertha L. Arrington, Judy Arrington Ball.

3. Information on the Fish family tree was given to me by the following persons: John Fish, Lou Ellen Russell Fish, Lawson Fish, Bertha Fish Morrow, William Marian Fish, and Laura Griffith Fish, and Albert Morrow. I also used the record that was written down in the Fish's family Bible.

5. Information on the Morrow family tree was given to me by the following persons: Albert Morrow, Victoria Morrow Jinkens, and Tommy Morrow.

6. Information on the Ford Family tree was given to me by the following persons: John Ike Ford and Lizzie Cynthia Ford.

7. Information on the Clark-Cole-Pierce family tree was given to me by the following persons: Robert Lemon Green, Nora Cogdill Pierce, Daniel Pierce, Frank Pierce, Anna Lee Pierce Fraley, Bonnie Kate Pierce Ford, Robert Lee Pierce, and Eliza Clark Pierce.

# Index

Griesel, G., 200
Griffen, J.,113
Griffith, Laura Aualine, 179, 180
Grindstaff, C., 21
Grooms, R., 110,140

Hagan, W., 36
Hagerman, Allen., 81,82
Hagerman, Jeffrey., 82
Hagerman, Steven, 81,82
Hall, Alvin, 96
Hall, Carl, 12,96
Hall, Robert, 177
Haney, W., 199
Harden, T., 31,34,37,130,135,136
*Harlan Daily Enterprise*, 125
Hat Greek, 12
Hays, R., 30,31
Henry, G., 61
Hixson, F. 38
Head, G., 37
Headley, T., 63
Henry, W., 79
Hensley, Emanuel., 1,9.14
Hensley, George Went,
    1,2,14,16,17,19,20,25,30,3,52,
    75-77, 81,116
Hensley, Johnny., 75
Hensley, Susan, 1,9,14,16
Holbrook, J., 78
Holden, F., 145
Holdway, J. C., 113
Hood, R., 149
Hooper, L., 116
Howes, G., 200
Hudd, B. Sr., 113
Hutton,O, 4,9,29,54,55,88,89

Ike, Bonnire, 184,185
Ike, John, 184,185

Jackson, Clint, 35,75
James, Cora, 96
James, Ethel, 103
Jane, L., 191

Jesus' Name, 5 ; Church(s), 21,
    130; Apostolic Church of God,
    71; Apostolic Church of God of
    the Lord Jesus, 70; Church of
    the Lord Jesus, 77; Church of
    the Lord Jesus Christ, 8;
    Church of God, 80,85; Church
    of God, Jesus' Name People,
    88; Church of the Lord Jesus,
    77,147; Church of the Lord
    Jesus Christ, 26, 147; Del-Rio
    Church of God in Jesus' Name,
    127; Edwina Church of God in
    Jesus Christ's Name,
    5.15,127,144; Faith Tabernacle
    in Jesus' Name, 126; Full
    Gospel Church of Jesus Christ,
    61; Full Gospel Tabernacle in
    Jesus' Name, 9,144; Holiness
    Church of God in Jesus' Name
    (Ga.), 8, 28-29; Holiness
    Church of God in Jesus' Name
    (Tn.),8, 39,40,57-
    59,60,61,105,107,109,110,113,115
    ,128; Holiness Church of God
    in Jesus' Name (Va.), 8, 21-23,
    61,63,86,87,103,138; House of
    Prayer in Jesus' Name,
    42,47,53,83,146,147; Mount
    Carmel House of Prayer in
    Jesus' Name, 73,83; Pineville
    Church of God, 11; Rock House
    Holiness Church,
    119,124,148,149; Sand Hill
    Church of God in Jesus' Name,
    44-45,50,95-
    100,103,104,112,113,115,137
Jesus'Name: Doctrine, 3,9,10, 14;
    Handlers, 43,57; People:
    Preacher 4,5; Preachers,
    1,6,7,11; Preaching, 14; Serpent
    handlers, 3,43,55; Serpent
    handling, 9,14; Snake handling,
    9
Jinkens, V.,200

# King James Bible Quotations